The Ascension of Isaiah

THE ASCENSION of ISAIAH

Jonathan Knight

Sheffield Academic Press

Copyright © 1995 Sheffield Academic Press

Published by Sheffield Academic Press Ltd
Mansion House
19 Kingfield Road
Sheffield, S11 9AS
England

Printed on acid-free paper in Great Britain
by The Cromwell Press
Melksham, Wiltshire

British Library Cataloguing in Publication Data

A catalogue record for this book is available
from the British Library

ISBN 1-85075-543-4

Contents

Preface		7
Abbreviations		8
1.	An Introduction to the Ascension of Isaiah	9
2.	The Setting of the Ascension of Isaiah	28
3.	A Commentary on the Ascension of Isaiah	47
4.	The Ascension of Isaiah and Themes in Early Christianity	79
General Bibliography		93
Index of References		98
Index of Authors		104

Preface

In recent years considerable attention has been given to the phenomenon of early Christian apocalyptic. The Ascension of Isaiah is a second-century apocalypse which reacts to the threat of Roman oppression and expresses concern that the experience of visionary contact with heaven was declining in early Christian communities. The author boldly expresses his hope for the Beloved One's return from heaven; but he also constructs a theory about what Jesus achieved on the cross which suggests that the need was felt to create a more detailed soteriology than is found in the New Testament literature.

This book is the result of several years' study and it has its origins in a doctoral dissertation which I submitted to the University of Cambridge in 1991. Many people have helped me in my work. Among them I should mention Dr Ernst Bammel, Professor Richard Bauckham and Professor Martin Hengel (who read a draft of some further work I have undertaken on this apocalypse). I am grateful to the Trustees of the Sir Henry Stephenson Fellowship at Sheffield University for providing me with the means to write this book. My biggest debt of gratitude, however, is to Professor Christopher Rowland. He encouraged and supervised my work from the very beginning and never failed to offer perceptive insights that stimulated my thought in a number of areas. This book is dedicated to him as a small token of what he has done.

List of Abbreviations

IEJ	*Israel Exploration Journal*
JBL	*Journal of Biblical Literature*
JSNT	*Journal for the Study of the New Testament*
JTS	*Journal of Theological Studies*
NTS	*New Testament Studies*
NTSup	*Novum Testamentum*, Supplement Series
SBLDS	SBL Dissertation Series
SJT	*Scottish Journal of Theology*
TDNT	*Theological Dictionary of the New Testament*

1
AN INTRODUCTION TO THE ASCENSION OF ISAIAH

The Ascension of Isaiah is a Jewish-Christian apocalypse which was written (so far as we know) in Syria between about 112 and 138 CE. An apocalypse is a work of literature which purports to describe the content of revealed heavenly mysteries, including eschatology and a variety of other topics (see the collection of essays on the genre edited by Collins, 1979). The term 'Jewish-Christian' identifies a form of Christian belief, found widely in the first two centuries CE, that was expressed in language and imagery derived from Judaism rather than from the Gentile world (for an introduction to Jewish Christianity see Daniélou 1964). The Ascension of Isaiah thus adopts the form of a revelatory work, familiar from earlier examples like the book of Daniel, and it claims to present revealed mysteries that would work for the benefit of readers. It is a Christian text written by someone who probably had a background in Judaism and who was accustomed to semitizing expressions and ideas which give his writing a distinctive character.

The Ascension of Isaiah is a pseudonymous apocalypse. Like many examples of the genre (Revelation is a notable exception) it was written long after the Old Testament writings but attributed to a well-known figure from Jewish history. The prophet Isaiah, who lived in the eighth century BCE, was chosen as the patron for this apocalypse because he was known to have seen God (Isa. 6) and had criticized powerful nations who opposed the faithful people of God (Isa. 13 and other references). The real author of the Ascension of Isaiah was not Isaiah himself but an unknown Christian writer in the second century CE. His own personality comes across briefly in passages such as 3.31

(the statement that prophetic oracles had been opposed) and perhaps in the description of the mystical ascension in ch. 6. Otherwise, however, he was the content to disguise his identity by using the fiction that the apocalypse was written by Isaiah. This literary device, which certainly did not deceive the earliest readers of the Ascension of Isaiah, had the effect of providing authority for the material presented in the apocalypse, specifically by suggesting that its prophecies of Beliar's downfall and security for Christians had been revealed in ancient times.

The Ascension of Isaiah falls into two halves. Chapters 1–5 contain a Christian eschatological prophecy of the last things (3.13–4.22) set within a narrative context which describes the prophet Isaiah's death (1.1–3.12, 5.1-16). The hope for the *parousia*, or return of Christ from heaven (4.14-18), and criticism of both the church leaders (3.21-31) and the Roman administration (4.1-13), are important features of this section. Chapter 6–11 describe Isaiah's mystical ascension to the seventh heaven in which he sees the heavenly Christ (who is called 'the Beloved One' in the Ascension of Isaiah) defeat the demon Beliar through his appearance on earth as Jesus. The relationship between the two halves of the Ascension of Isaiah has been much discussed in the past but the most recent scholarship accepts that the work was written by a single author who had a definite purpose in mind.

If we probe into the material we can see that the Ascension of Isaiah comes from an author who was conscious of insecurity in the world around him. 3.13–4.22 (a passage which is called 'the First Vision' in this Guide) shows that this person felt threatened by more powerful Christians (3.21-31), who are evidently the church leaders, and by the activity of the Roman government (4.1-13). The status of prophecy was an important issue in his relations with the church leaders. 2.7-11 presents the prophets as isolated people and 3.26-27 notes the paucity of prophets in the church, while 3.31 hints that the author had himself been opposed by the leaders. 3.21-31, taken together with the work's narrative portions, suggests that the author was a member of a circle that included prophets at a time when prophecy was beginning to lose its appeal in the church. The understanding of prophecy which the Ascension of Isaiah upholds is shown by chs. 6–11 to have had a strong mystical element which evidently involved 'extra-bodily' experience in which the mystic thought that he journeyed to the throne of God.

Additionally, the author expresses what must have been a general feeling of resentment at the fact of Roman domination (4.1-13) Christians had a specific cause for resentment towards the Romans in the early second century because they were subjected to sporadic official persecution at that time. An important example of this is the situation in Bithynia (in Asia Minor) in 112 CE which is described in a letter written by the governor Pliny to the emperor Trajan in Rome (*Ep.* 10.96). Pliny explains that he had come across Christians in his province and had determined a test of their loyalty to the state by requiring them to offer incense before statues of Trajan and the gods and to curse Christ. The First Vision seems to reflect knowledge of this situation in Bithynia, and its author criticizes Rome for demanding worship (ch. 4) and for killing people who resisted that demand (ch. 5). The First Vision is essentially a reassuring statement that the Beloved One would soon return from heaven to bring such oppression to an end and it voices the hope that the righteous would share the mediator's earthly reign (4.14-18).

Chapters 6–11 (which are called 'the Second Vision' in this Guide) have a more timeless perspective than the First Vision although they take their terms of reference from the first half of the Ascension of Isaiah. The situation addressed in the second half of the work is the same as in the first but the solution offered to it is different. This situation is one in which insecurity is the dominant factor and in which the author attributes the problems of his life to the arrogant behaviour of Beliar, the chief demon in the firmament (the region between earth and the seven heavens) who inspired the Romans. The Second Vision constructs a mythological drama in which the author's hope for security is expressed in a description of how the Beloved One defeated these aerial powers. Beliar is said to be struggling with his angels in the firmament and the author implies that his striving determined human conflict (7.9-12). The Beloved's descent from the seventh heaven, which forms the main part of the Second Vision, resulted in the demon's 'judgment and destruction' (words used in 10.12) and alleviated this problem. The Ascension of Isaiah concludes with a description of the Beloved's ascension to the seventh heaven and his enthronement at the right hand of God (11.23-33). This is a way of demonstrating that Beliar had been defeated. The purpose of the Second Vision was to reassure readers that the Beloved had intervened decisively in their dilemma by defeating Beliar on the cross, so that hope was possible even though the circumstances of their lives may have seemed bleak.

Christianity in the Second Century

An important feature of the Ascension of Isaiah is the light that it sheds on Christianity in the second century CE. This is a period about which relatively little is known. Following the deaths of the first Christian generation, which must have happened almost without exception by the end of the first century CE, people were faced with the task of preserving their faith without the help of people like Peter and Paul, and they had to adjust to a situation in which hopes for Jesus' return from heaven were beginning to seem obsolete. The little that we know about this period, mainly from 1 Clement (c. 96 CE) and the letters of Ignatius (c. 110 CE), suggests that struggles for authority took place in Christian churches and that leaders were sometimes ousted (see 1 Clem. 44; and Schoedel 1985: 13-14 on the situation addressed by Ignatius). There were also disputes about the significance of Jesus in which some claimed that his humanity was extraordinary and that he did not really die on the cross. These people were called 'docetists', from the Greek word *dokein* which means 'to seem'.

The Ascension of Isaiah offers an insight into this period but its evidence has often been neglected. The text has much in common with the New Testament writings, some of which its author apparently knew, and it represents a development of their ideas. An important area in which this is so is eschatology. The Ascension of Isaiah preserves the hope that the returning Christ would reign on earth (4.14-18) which is found in 1 Cor. 15.24-25 and Rev. 20.4 and is often called the 'millenarian' hope; but the apocalypse adds to this the Second Vision which offers a more theoretical or systematic account of what the Beloved One had already achieved. It is difficult to comment on the issue of authorial intention but material in chs. 6–11 looks like a way of creating hope should the Beloved *fail* to return just as much as it offers hope for the period before the *parousia*. The failure of *parousia* hopes was a situation which first-century Christianity had not anticipated. The author's interest in what Jesus had achieved was one of the ways in which second-century Christianity reacted to the initial disappointment of its eschatological hopes. This was done by creating a body of doctrine that seemed relevant to the needs of a changing world and which insisted that everything needed for salvation had already been provided.

The Ascension of Isaiah also offers information about the social history of the early second century. It describes how the church leaders fell out with one another in their desire for personal advancement (3.21-31). This evidence can be confirmed from the letters of Ignatius (the bishop of Antioch who was killed in Rome c. 110 CE) which suggest that Ignatius himself was aware of people who wanted his job (see Schoedel 1985: 10-11). The Ascension of Isaiah further indicates that prophecy was falling into decline at this time (see 2.7-11, 3.27-28 and 6.14-17). Prophecy had been a mainstay of first-century Christianity and Paul's Corinthian letters (especially 1 Cor. 12–14) show the hold which it exercised there. The book of Revelation indicates that primitive Christian prophecy had an apocalyptic dimension which was bound up with mystical experience of the heavenly world. The Ascension of Isaiah describes a situation in which prophets, in this case evidently people with such an apocalyptic interest, had apparently become marginalized figures (2.7-11) who suffered repression from the more powerful leaders (3.31). This was related in some way to the rise of institutional leadership in second-century Christianity.

Scholarly neglect of the Ascension of Isaiah is thus by no means a true reflection of the work's importance. The text repays careful study by everyone interested in the history of early Christianity and indeed in Jewish pseudepigraphal literature. It is almost a unique text in offering a sustained account of Christ's incarnation and atonement (chs. 6–11) at a time when Christianity was undergoing rapid change and development. It holds an interest for a range of issues in the study of late antiquity.

The Accessibility of the Text

Perhaps the most difficult problem faced by readers of the Ascension of Isaiah is the fact that the text now exists only in a number of later translations, in languages as diverse as Ethiopic and Slavonic. This difficulty is compounded by the fact that there is no satisfactory critical edition of the text. A new edition is being prepared in Italy but its publication date has not been announced.

This problem affects readers of this Guide inasmuch as all the available English translations are based on incomplete manuscript evidence. Of those published the translation by M.A. Knibb (1985) is to be preferred because it works from the most complete selection of manuscripts and alone represents a fresh collation of that evidence. Knibb includes valuable footnotes and textual comments which will help anyone who wants to gain a detailed knowledge of the apocalypse.

Knibb's translation was used in the preparation of this Guide, and his correction of the Ethiopic text with reference to the other versions is generally followed here.

Reading the Ascension of Isaiah: A Survey of its Contents

The Ascension of Isaiah contains three different kinds of material: narrative traditions about Isaiah, the First Vision (3.13–4.22) and the Second Vision (chs. 6–11). The Second Vision circulated independently in one branch of the textual tradition (a Latin translation and the Slavonic translation) and the natural break between chs. 5 and 6 was recognized at some point in antiquity.

Scholarship in the early part of this century thought that the Ascension of Isaiah was written in a 'scissors and paste' method (so Charles 1900) in which the author combined a number of earlier documents to yield the finished apocalypse. More recent research (presented initially at a 1981 conference) has convincingly argued that the apocalypse was written as a whole and that, while there were a number of sources, the author must be seen as a creative individual who shaped his traditions in a way that had a definite setting and purpose (see Pesce 1983). The tendency of this research, which was undertaken by the Italian team who are preparing the new edition, is to reject any approach that dissects the apocalypse into 'earlier documents'. This is the view adopted in this Guide. It means that the theory, proposed by Charles (1900) and supported recently by Knibb (1985), that one of the sources for the work was a Jewish narrative text called the Martyrdom of Isaiah is rejected here.

The Ascension of Isaiah begins by describing a meeting between Hezekiah and Manasseh at which Isaiah and his son were present as witnesses. Hezekiah warned Manasseh about his future behaviour (1.1-6) but Isaiah counselled that this would have no effect (1.7-9). This warning is amply fulfilled in ch. 2. Manasseh is said to have been possessed by Sammael (one of the names for the demon Beliar) and to have turned away from Hezekiah's piety (2.1). Isaiah was distressed by such lawlessness, which he observed first in Jerusalem and then again in Bethlehem, and he withdrew to the desert where he founded an ascetic community (2.7-8). Those who joined him were given the names of prophets. They dressed in sackcloth, ate only vegetables, and 'lamented' over Israel's apostasy (2.9-11). This story evidently had a meaning which the author held important for his readers, although it would be wrong to see it as an *allegory* of their situation. It has much in common with 3.21-31, where the author describes how the prophets were opposed by 'wicked shepherds and elders'.

The Isaianic community were harried at their retreat by a false prophet called Belchira who visited them there (ch. 3). Belchira next denounced Isaiah before Manasseh. He made three allegations against the prophet: that Isaiah had predicted the destruction of Jerusalem and the cities of Judah (3.6); that he had claimed to have seen God when Moses said that this was impossible (3.8-10a); and that he had compared the Jerusalem authorities to the rulers of Sodom and Gomorrah (3.10b). As a result of these charges Isaiah was arrested and brought before Manasseh (3.12).

The charge that Isaiah falsely claimed to have seen God (3.8-10a) introduces the First Vision which begins in 3.13. The First Vision is a Christian eschatological prophecy which surveys the course of history from the ministry of Jesus to his expected *parousia*. It takes the form of an apocalyptic historical review of a kind found in Daniel and other apocalyptic writings (see Collins 1977: 158-62). This device looks back on earlier history in a critical way and it posits an imminent supernatural intervention through which the ills of the present would be redressed. The author of the Ascension of Isaiah specifies four periods before the Beloved One's *parousia*. These periods are: (1) the ministry of Jesus (3.13-18); (2) the apostolic age (3.19-20); (3) the post-apostolic period (3.21-31); and (4) the period of Roman domination (4.1-13). These would be followed by (5) the millenarian kingdom, when the Beloved One would return from heaven to begin his reign on earth (4.14-18). While there is a sense of development in the scheme, notably in the author's conviction that the apostolic age lay in the past (3.21), we should not necessarily expect to find a precise historical account there. The author states that things had deteriorated after the apostles died (3.21). This is his way of commenting on what he took to be the difficulties of the post-apostolic period. The First Vision addresses a double-edged situation in which opposition towards the prophets by the church leaders and harassment of Christians by the Romans had created a profound sense of despair.

The ministry of Jesus is described in language which shows knowledge of Matthew's special material (3.13-18) and of broader traditions as well (cf. also '11.2-22 in the Ethiopic text'). Jesus is presented as the earthly appearance of the Beloved One who had descended from the seventh heaven and assumed human form. The noun 'transformation' (into human form), used in 3.13, shows the character of the christology as a heavenly mediator's temporary epiphany. Descent (3.13) and ascension (3.18) are prominent categories in this work, as they are in one strand of Johannine christology (see Jn 3.13; 6.62) with which the Ascension of Isaiah holds ideas in common.

The ministry of Jesus is followed in the author's historical review by the apostolic age (3.19-20). He claims that people spoke by the Holy Spirit at this time and that many signs and miracles were done. The conviction that the apostolic age lay in the past is strongly expressed in the Ascension of Isaiah (3.21). The author looks back on this bygone age as a time of charismatic prowess which contrasted with what he held to be the withdrawal of the Holy Spirit from his own generation (3.26-28).

The author describes his own day in 3.21-31. He states that people 'had' begun to forget what the apostles had taught and how they had lived (3.21). 3.21-31 attacks a group of fellow Christians on the grounds that they were greedy and ambitious people who vied with each other for office. The phrase 'wicked elders and shepherds' used in 3.24 strongly implies that the *church leaders* are criticized here. The author seems to have been suspicious of the emerging orders of ministry to the extent that these were taking the place of the prophets in second-century Christianity.

Three passages from the wider section 3.21-31 reveal the basis of the author's complaint against the leaders. 3.25 says that many would 'exchange the garments of the saints for the robes of those who loved money' and that there would be 'much respect of persons in those days, and lovers of the glory of the world'. This reveals a situation in which the desire for social improvement was a prominent feature. 3.26b states that the Holy Spirit would withdraw from many and 3.27-28 notes the disappearance of prophecy at the time except for a few isolated individuals (cf. 2.7-11). 3.31 then mentions an attempt to 'make ineffective' the prophets and Isaiah's own prophecy. The pseudonymity seems to recede at this point to reveal the author's own identity as a prophet who had been opposed by the church leaders, but nothing is said to indicate what this repression involved.

4.1-13 shows a further aspect of the author's unease by mentioning the domineering attitude of Rome towards Christian people at the time. The language used here is allusive but it is possible to discern something of the situation which prompted the apocalypse. The Ascension of Isaiah uses the myth of Nero's return, a myth which is found in other literature, to present Rome as the embodiment of demonic forces in that the demon Beliar is said to have descended from the firmament in the form of Nero (cf. also Sib. Or. 3.63-74). The author was not so much expecting Nero's return (although rumours about this persisted for a long time after the emperor's death in 68 CE) as using a traditional form of imagery to describe Rome's harassment of pious Christians in the second century. 4.3 looks back to the Neronian Persecution (64 CE) and states (in the Greek text) that one of the twelve (the Ethiopic says 'some') would be delivered into his hand. Most scholars take this as a reference to Peter's martyrdom in Rome on that occasion (cf. also 1 Clem. 5.4; Ign. Rom. 4.3).

It is argued in this Guide that the Ascension of Isaiah was written with a knowledge of what had befallen the Christians of Bithynia in about 112 CE. We possess a letter written at the time by Pliny, the governor of that province, to the emperor Trajan in Rome asking for instructions about what to do with Christians who had come to notice in his territory (*Ep.* 10. 96; translation in Stevenson 1987: 18-21). Pliny reported that they had been denounced in an anonymous pamphlet and that he had examined them but found no evidence for criminal activity. His procedure, so he says, was to ask them first of all whether they were Christians, then again a second and a third time with threats of punishment. If they persisted in their belief they were executed for stubbornness, except those who were Roman citizens. Those who were arrested but denied the charge were given a test of their loyalty to the state. They were required to offer wine and incense before the statues of Trajan and the gods and to curse Christ. This was something which Pliny noted that pious Christians would refuse to do. Pliny also states that he had examined Christians who had given up their belief some years ago, so that the possibility of apostasy (mentioned by Asc. Isa. 4.9) was apparently a real one at the time. This test of loyalty which Pliny imposed in Bithynia will be referred to in this Guide as the 'sacrifice test'.

Trajan's reply broadly commended Pliny for his policy (Pliny, *Ep.* 10. 97; translation in Stevenson 1987: 20-21) and agreed that he had adopted a proper course of action. The emperor added that Christians were not to be sought out for investigation in this way, least of all by anonymous pamphleteering. If, however, they were properly accused and were found to be guilty they were liable for punishment. Trajan also upheld the validity of the sacrifice test. His reply cleared the way for Pliny's procedure to become standard practice in other parts of the empire, We know from the later Martyrdom of Polycarp (mid-second century CE) that Polycarp was asked to swear by the genius of Caesar and to curse Christ before he was martyred (see Stevenson 1987: 25-26). This seems very similar to the requirement which Pliny had imposed, as if usage of the test had spread beyond Bithynia.

The assumption that the author of the Ascension of Isaiah knew of this or of a similar encounter with the Roman authorities would explain the form of the material in the middle part of ch. 4. That section of the chapter describes how Beliar was incarnated as a Roman emperor. Beliar is made to say 'I am the LORD, and before me there was no one' (4.6). This statement is a parody of Isa. 45.18 (where the words are spoken by God) and its implication is that Rome had usurped God's own place in demanding homage. It is followed by the comment in 4.8 that people would 'sacrifice to him and serve him', where the reference to 'sacrifice' calls to mind the test which Pliny had imposed. 4.11 then says that 'he will set his image before him in every city' which again suits the Bithynian situation. We do not know whether Christians in Syria had experienced the same kind of investigation as their Bithynian counterparts. It is not impossible that they had, but perhaps the Ascension of Isaiah is better explained as a reaction to the sudden spread of rumours that investigation of this kind was impending.

The First Vision represents a response to the difficulties described in this way. The author's historical review culminates in the hope that the Beloved's expected return from heaven would inaugurate his reign on earth. The returning Beloved One was expected to drag Beliar and his hosts to Gehenna (4.14) and provide 'rest' for those who had shown themselves faithful under conflict (4.15). Even the departed would 'descend from heaven with the Lord' (4.16) so that death was not a barrier to participation in the kingdom. Following an unspecified period on earth all the faithful would ascend to a glorious heavenly immortality (4.17). This would be followed by a judgment in which the Beloved 'rebuked' everything that had supported Beliar's tyranny (4.18).

Chapter 5 describes how Isaiah was put to death by Manasseh. The death penalty had recently been imposed on Christians by Romans (Pliny, *Ep*. 10.96; cf. Rev. 2.13 which comes from the reign of Domitian) and this seems to be the situation reflected here. The martyrdom of Ignatius (c. 110 CE) would have been an outstanding recent example of what such 'conflict' might bring. The author praises

1. An Introduction to the Ascension of Isaiah

the courage of a prophet who refused to recant his faith and bravely endured suffering for the sake of his Christian belief.

Chapter 6 introduces the second half of the apocalypse, which is called 'the Second Vision' in this Guide. The second vision presents a self-contained account of Isaiah's mystical ascension to the seventh heaven. Chapter 6 offers a valuable description of the preparations for mystical experience in the ancient Jewish world, something about which Jewish and Christian writers were generally reluctant to speak (see 2 Cor. 12) and which was subjected to careful controls in the early Common Era (see Rowland 1982a: 306-48). The author states that Isaiah's body remained inert on the ground, evidently in some form of cataleptic trance, while the prophet thought that he ascended through the heavens to witness the Beloved One's descent and ascension. The Ascension of Isaiah is one of the few ancient Jewish sources to describe this 'extra-bodily' experience with relative clarity.

The substance of the Second Vision, recorded in chs. 7–11, is a description of how the Beloved One gained his victory over Beliar. While much of the material is christological (describing what the Beloved One had done) this christology has both a soteriological and an eschatological aspect. Its purpose was to reassure readers who felt threatened in their environment by insisting that the Beloved had already achieved what was needed for their security. It does this by introducing a cosmology that posits seven heavens above the earth. A number of Jewish apocalypses describe a sequence of heavens (typically seven) in this way but the Ascension of Isaiah seems to be exceptional in early Christian literature in doing so. According to this scheme the Beloved sat enthroned with God and the Spirit in the seventh heaven (11.32-33) while Beliar was excluded from the heavens and inhabited only the firmament (7.9-12). This was a way of showing readers how far their patron transcended the demon who was inspiring Roman opposition to the Christians. The author's interest in this material falls on Isaiah's mystical journey to the seventh heaven (chs. 7–9) and on his vision of the Beloved's saving activity (chs. 10–11).

Chapter 7 makes an important statement about Beliar's fate. Following the hint that the demon's behaviour was the cause of human strife (7.10; cf. 4.4) the author makes the point that Beliar's striving would last until the Beloved One came to destroy him (7.12). As had been said in ch. 4 this makes the Beloved's intervention the cause of salvation.

Chapters 7 and 8 describe Isaiah's ascension through the heavens.

Chapter 9 narrates how he entered the seventh heaven and saw the Beloved One and the angel of the Holy Spirit as they were worshipped by the angels there (9.27-36), and how they in turn led the angels in the worship of God (9.40-42). The Beloved's journey to earth is described in chs. 10 and 11. 10.6-17 claims to present the words of God which instructed the Beloved to descend from the seventh heaven so that he might 'judge and destroy' the angels who were acting arrogantly in the firmament. This passage supplies the reason for the descent in the angels' refusal to acknowledge God (cf. 7.9-12). The crucial moment in this judgment, so 10.13-14 implies, was the Beloved One's death on the cross. 10.14 includes the words '*afterwards* you shall ascend from the gods of death to your place' in a context where the 'afterwards' denotes the resurrection, so that the author's interest apparently rests with the crucifixion as the decisive saving moment (cf. Col. 2.15).

10.17-30 describes how the Beloved left the seventh heaven and descended towards the earth. He changed his appearance to resemble that of the angels in the different heavens so that these did not recognize or worship him. In this way he journeyed through the firmament and escaped the notice of the angels there.

Chapter 11 describes how he appeared on earth as Jesus. There is a textual problem at this point but the longer version found in the Ethiopic text (11.2-22) describes how the Beloved was transformed into the human Jesus in the womb of Mary and lived out his life on earth. This section includes further material in common with Matthew's Gospel (cf. 3.13-18). The apocalypse is not free from a form of docetism, the tendency to attribute superhuman properties to Jesus, in which Mary had a short pregnancy and Jesus did not really need suckling (see 11.7-8, 17), but the Ascension of Isaiah insists that he really died on the cross (11.19-20).

The Beloved One rose from the grave and ascended to heaven (11.22-33). In his ascension he revealed his identity as the divine subordinate to the angels and was worshipped by these when they saw him. The first angels to offer worship in this way were the rebellious ones in the firmament, who asked how they had failed to recognize 'their Lord' when he passed them in the descent. There is a textual problem in 11.23-24 in which the Beloved is held to ascend directly from the firmament to the second heaven, but this must not be allowed to obscure the fact that the angels in the firmament were in all probability the first to offer him worship in this way. This was a sign of

1. An Introduction to the Ascension of Isaiah

their submission and it reflects the fact of their defeat which had been accomplished on the cross. The Beloved's ascension to the throne of God was thus that of a mediator who had already proved victorious in his conflict with demonic powers.

At the high point of his ascension the Beloved sat on a throne to the right of the throne of God (11.32). The Holy Spirit is said to be seated on the left (11.33). The prophet's vision of the Beloved's enthronement was also the moment of his dismissal from heaven, which seems to be the author's way of saying that everything that he wished to disclose about the achievement of salvation had by then been revealed. The Ascension of Isaiah concludes with some further traditions about Isaiah which make the point that the apocalypse was written for the 'final generation' (11.37-38), which the author evidently saw as his own.

The Date and Provenance of the Ascension of Isaiah

It is difficult to date the Ascension of Isaiah with precision but helpful to specify some parameters which can determine any decision. It is argued here that the correspondence between Pliny and Trajan in c. 112 CE explains many of the allusions in the First Vision. This means that the apocalypse was probably not written before the second decade of the second century CE, but it is difficult to say how much later than this it appeared. Perhaps a few years must be allowed for Pliny's procedure to have been adopted by governors in other parts of the Roman empire. Given that the First Vision alludes to the myth of Nero's return (4.4), as does Book 5 of the Sibylline Oracles (see below), the material may have been written as late as the Second Jewish Revolt against Rome (132–135 CE) but probably not later than the death of Hadrian (138 CE). A number of differences from the Gnostic literature indicate that the Ascension of Isaiah was written before 150 CE, the date of the earliest Gnostic writings. The apocalypse may thus provisionally be assigned to the period 112–138 CE, and it may possibly comes from the period before the Second Revolt.

Direct internal evidence for the date is not very extensive. The First Vision could not have been written before the Neronian Persecution (64 CE) to which it alludes in 4.3, and in fact it is considerably later than this. The conviction that the apostolic age had past and been succeeded by a later period (3.21) suggests the late first century CE as the earliest possible date, and more likely indeed the second century.

This is confirmed by the material describing Rome's opposition to pious Christians in chs. 4 and 5, which can be explained with reference to the correspondence between Pliny and Trajan and which sets the Ascension of Isaiah after about 112 CE. Pliny's letter suggests that there had been a number of martyrs, whereas we know of only one person who died in the so-called 'Persecution' under Domitian (the Antipas mentioned by Rev. 2.13). The author of the Ascension of Isaiah's sense that prophecy was declining, his use of the New Testament writings, and the utopian eschatology of chs. 6–11 all suit a situation in the second century when Christianity was coming to terms with its sense of distance from the apostolic age and with the need to reformulate its hopes about salvation.

Two passages have sometimes been used to date the work earlier than this. These are the allusion to the myth of Nero's return in ch. 4 and the belief that 4.13 implies that some of the first generation of Christians were still alive. It should not be assumed that rumours about Nero's return ceased within a few decades of his death. While they certainly circulated within months of his suicide in 68 CE, mythology anticipating Nero's return is a prominent theme in the Sibylline Oracles, especially in Book 5 where the relevant portion comes from the reign of Hadrian (Sib. Or. 5.101-104). This means that the Ascension of Isaiah cannot be confined to the first century because of what it states about Nero's reincarnation. Such mythology continued to circulate at the time of the Second Jewish Revolt (132–135 CE), more than sixty years after Nero had died.

The second passage is Asc. Isa 4.13. The text of this is corrupt but it apparently says that:

> Many faithful and saints, when they saw him for whom they were hoping, who was crucified, Jesus the Lord Christ—after I, Isaiah had seen him who was crucified and ascended—and who believed in him, of these few will be left in those days as his servants.

We cannot be certain that the Ethiopic offers a precise translation of the Greek at this point. Elsewhere in the apocalypse 'Jesus' is said to be a name appropriate only to the Beloved's earthly manifestation (9.5; 10.7) and the combination of titles 'Jesus the Lord Christ' is unique in this form in the Ascension of Isaiah (although the phrase 'Lord Jesus Christ' is found frequently in the New Testament writings). This makes it possible that the author inserted part of 4.13 from a source. Although the verse does seem to refer to the original eyewitnesses of

Jesus, its main focus is not the fact that some ('few') of these were alive when the apocalypse was written but that 'few' Christians were left '*as his servants*'. The author is commenting on the small numbers of Christians who remained faithful in the last days, not primarily on the number of those original eyewitnesses still alive at the time of writing. In the light of 3.21-22, which shows the author's clear sense of distance from the apostolic age, the apparent admission that 'few' who had seen Jesus were alive should perhaps be taken as hyperbole, so that the phrase constitutes an admission that *all* the original Christian generation had died. This tends to support a date for the Ascension of Isaiah in the period to which this Guide assigns it.

The provenance of the Ascension of Isaiah is by general consent Syria. This is accepted by commentators with the exception of Bori (1980), who argues that it was written in Asia because of the similarities with Montanism. The use of Isaiah traditions, the description of heavenly ascension in chs. 6–11, the reference to Tyre and Sidon in 5.13, and the possibility that the Isaiah traditions once circulated in Hebrew (mentioned by Knibb 1985: 146-47) all point to an origin in the Syro-Palestine area. The work testifies to the history of Christianity in that region in the period after the martyrdom of Ignatius.

The Textual Evidence for the Ascension of Isaiah

One reason why the Ascension of Isaiah has been neglected in the past is because of its difficult textual problems. Although it was probably written in Greek it survives now for the most part only in a number of later translations, so that specialists in several disciplines are needed to make it accessible.

Fragments of the apocalypse are extant in a Greek version (Gk). The text was discovered by Grenfell and Hunt in a papyrological collection at the beginning of the century; it covers 2.4–4.4 with occasional lacunae (text in Charles 1900: 84-95; see also Knibb 1985: 144-46 on all the versions). There is also a medieval Greek recasting called the Greek Legend (GL) which offers an abbreviated version of ch. 1 of the Ascension of Isaiah but which then places a reworked version of chs. 6–11 before material found in chs. 2–5 (for the text see Charles 1900: 141-48). The Greek Legend clearly alters the original: it resolves the chronological problem between 1.1 and 6.1 and shows signs of conformity to the New Testament in some of its readings (see e.g. GL 2.25). Both Greek versions confirm that, in those places where it can be tested against them, the Ethiopic is an essentially reliable though at times a rather wooden translation (cf. 9.5). It is reassuring to discover that the Ethiopic does not obviously contain wild idiosyncrasies, but this is not to say that it is accurate at every point.

The Ethiopic version (E) was produced in the fourth or fifth century CE but it now exists in manuscripts at least a millennium younger. The Ethiopian church greatly valued the apocalyptic literature and preserved the Ascension of Isaiah together with other texts like 1 Enoch (see Ullendorff 1968; Metzger 1977: 215-23). The Ethiopic text of the Ascension of Isaiah is preserved in seven manuscripts. Only the first three of these were available to Charles and all but the last two to Knibb, whose translation represents a fresh collation of that evidence. A *full* collation and assessment of this evidence awaits the new edition. Along with the Coptic (and probably the Gk) the Ethiopic provides evidence that the Ascension of Isaiah originally included *both* the apocalyptic visions.

The apocalypse is also known through two Latin translations (L1 and L2). These are of different character and scope. L1 covers 2.14–3.13 and 7.1-19 and has close affinities with E. It was found in a Vatican palimpsest and has been re-edited by C. Leonardi (text in Charles 1900: 87-92). Despite some differences between them E, Gk and L1 all represent essentially the same textual tradition. This is obvious in 7.1-19 where E and L1 generally agree together against L2 and the Slavonic version (S) in reporting the early stages of Isaiah's ascension.

L2 is quite different from L1 and represents a separate branch of the textual tradition (text in Charles 1900: 98-139). It was published in 1522 by the Venetian printer A. de Fantis, from a manuscript now unknown, and republished by Gieseler in 1832. It covers only chs. 6–11 which it introduces with the title '*Visio, quam vidit Isaias propheta, filius Amos*'. A similar title is found also in S which also reproduces only chs. 6–11. The reason for this agreement seems to be that both versions were based on an abbreviated text of the Ascension of Isaiah which circulated in the patristic period. L2 often agrees with S against E, most notably in ch. 11 where these versions omit the Jesus traditions found in 11.2-22 (E), but there are important differences between L2 and S which should not be minimized (see e.g. 7.7-8).

The Slavonic version comes from the eleventh century. It exists in two forms, the second of which is an abbreviation of the first. The complete version is known from a twelfth–century Russian manuscript and from other later manuscripts. A Latin translation of the Slavonic version, prepared by Bonwetsch, was included in Charles' edition (1900: 98-139), but A. Vaillant has noticed some inaccuracies in this. The relation between S and L2 is a matter of dispute (see Knibb 1985: 145-46).

L2 and S raise a difficult textual problem in study of the Ascension of Isaiah. They reproduce *only* chs. 6–11 and show that this material at some stage circulated independently of the rest. The Second Vision is reproduced there in a form which displays significant differences from E, notably in ch. 11 where the traditions about Jesus are omitted. Their tendency towards abbreviation is evident throughout chs. 6-11. An example of this is in ch. 6 where both shorten the description of Isaiah's mystical ascension as if this were viewed with suspicion. The different versions of ch. 6 have been studied by Bori (1980), who concludes that L2 and S drew on a redaction of the apocalypse that was made at some point after the Montanist controversy and that their parent abbreviated the text because the original author had equated prophecy with charismatic experience—a view which the church decisively rejected at that time.

Doctrinal considerations also explain the other abbreviations made by this (lost) parent of S and L2. 11.2-22 was evidently omitted because of its docetic tendencies and chs. 1–5 because of their millenarian eschatology. Millenarianism—the belief that the resurrected would reign on earth with the messiah—was held increasingly suspect in the patristic period (see Bietenhard 1953). L2 and S must therefore be used with care as a source for the Ascension of Isaiah, but occasionally they provide access to the lost original when the Ethiopic translator nods or errs (e.g. 9.3).

Fragments of the apocalypse are found also in the Sahidic and Akhmimic dialects of Coptic. The Coptic translation supports the Ethiopic in including both halves of the Ascension of Isaiah.

The Sources of the Apocalypse

A conference on the Ascension of Isaiah held in Rome in 1981 provided the opportunity for some fresh thinking about the composition of the apocalypse. This was the first work of substance undertaken on the Ascension of Isaiah since R.H. Charles published his edition at the beginning of the present century. The conference offered substantial criticism of many of his views.

Charles had seen the author of the Ascension of Isaiah as essentially an editor who compiled his apocalypse from existing documents. This was typical of the approach which scholars of that generation adopted to the apocalyptic literature as a whole. Charles thought that this person worked in the second or third century CE and that he created the apocalypse from three different works: the Testament of Hezekiah, the Martyrdom of Isaiah and the Vision of Isaiah. Charles thought that these texts probably existed in the first century (1900: xxxvi-xliii). The Martyrdom of Isaiah supposedly contained the narrative of Isaiah's death and the Testament of Hezekiah (3.13–4.22—material called 'the First Vision' here) the substance of the conversation between Hezekiah and Manasseh in ch. 1. Charles's Vision of Isaiah was chs. 6–11 of the Ascension of Isaiah.

There are several problems with this theory, not least the observation that 3.13–4.22 is really a Christian eschatological prophecy that is attributed pseudonymously to Isaiah. This makes it difficult to suppose that the First Vision was originally a Testament of Hezekiah. Pesce also criticized the identification of a written Martyrdom of Isaiah on the grounds that the Talmud preserves rabbinic traditions about Isaiah in two completely different forms (1983: 28, 40-48; see *b. Yeb.* 49b and *b. Sanh.* 103b; cp. *y. Sanh.* 10.2). These are combined in the Ascension of Isaiah and this suggests that the Isaiah material was derived from oral tradition rather than from a written document. This rejection of the theory of a written Martyrdom, Testament and Vision in the most recent scholarship explains the titles for 3.13–4.22 and chs. 6–11 ('the First Vision' and 'the Second Vision') which are used in this Guide. These are intended to identify the relevant sections of the apocalypse but without offering a preconceived view of their authorship.

The question arises of how and why the Ascension of Isaiah was written. The view taken here is that a single author wrote it for a definite purpose. The work has a coherent theme, despite several awkward transitions. The purpose of the Ascension of Isaiah was to encourage a circle in the early second century CE that included a number of prophets who were disturbed by the state of church life and by recent developments in the Christian relationship with Rome. The author dealt with these problems by providing assurance about the millenarian hope and by drawing attention to what the Beloved One had already achieved. The apocalypse was written to create hope through this combination of ideas.

Further Reading

The understanding of 'apocalyptic' in the early Common Era
There has been a dispute in scholarship as to whether 'apocalyptic' denotes a 'transcendent eschatology' or more generally an 'interest in discerning heavenly secrets'. The former view is held by Hanson (1979). Hanson believes that 'apocalyptic eschatology' originated in the disillusionment of a visionary group who conflicted with the priests following the Israelite return from exile. Hanson's exegesis of certain post-exilic texts, especially of deutero-Zechariah, has been questioned by subsequent scholars, as for instance by Larkin (1994). An increasing body of opinion now associates the origins of apocalyptic with the tradition of mantic wisdom in Israel. One of the problems with Hanson's understanding when it is applied to the apocalyptic literature is the existence of several non-eschatological sections in the extant apocalypses which display an interest in the revelation of heavenly secrets that is broader than eschatology alone. These passages have been identified and examined by Stone (1976: 414-54). This broader understanding of apocalyptic as mysticism is adopted by many scholars including Rowland (1982: 7-48).

Jewish Christianity
This Guide takes the view that the Ascension of Isaiah comes from an author who retained Jewish ways of thought long after Gentile Christianity had come to be the dominant force in the church. Daniélou (1964) offers the most comprehensive introduction to the subject of Jewish Christianity and he often discusses the Ascension of Isaiah. See also Longenecker (1970); Dunn (1990: 235-66;) and the examination of the subject by G. Strecker in the Appendix to Bauer (1972: 241-85). Patristic reports about the Jewish-Christian sectarians are examined by Klijn and Reininck (1973).

The history of Christianity in the second century
The history of the period under discussion is examined by Chadwick (1967: 23-31); Frend (1991: 35-48; 1986: 147-51).

Other early Christian literature mentioned in this chapter
There is a translation of Ignatius, 1 Clement and the Didache in Staniforth (1987). There is a commentary on Ignatius by Schoedel (1985). An interesting collection of primary sources dealing with Roman persecution of Christians is offered in Stevenson (1987).

2

THE SETTING OF THE ASCENSION OF ISAIAH

This Guide will now proceed by examining the setting of the Ascension of Isaiah in more detail. It is necessary to study the author's sense of unease with the world about him in order to understand the response which the two Visions represent. Perhaps the best way to do this is to begin by asking whom the author of the Ascension of Isaiah presents as his opponents.

Hostility towards Judaism

The first point to be considered is the author's hostility towards Judaism. The apocalypse criticizes Judaism in several ways. First of all it says that the Jews were responsible for tormenting and betraying Jesus (3.13; 11.19). Secondly, the first and third of Belchira's charges against Isaiah (3.6-10) present the destruction of Jerusalem as an event that had been predicted by the prophet. This would have had an unmistakable relevance in a Christian text written after 70 CE and it suggests that what had happened to the Jewish capital was both within the divine plan and perhaps even divine punishment. Thirdly, 3.9-10 and 4.21-22 by implication devalue the religious insight of Moses and of Jews who read the Torah.

This third point needs a little explanation. The Torah is not cited with approval anywhere in the Ascension of Isaiah. The strong implication of 3.8-10 and 4.21-22 is that the author did not think that Moses had predicted the advent of the Beloved One. 3.8-10 allows that Isaiah enjoyed mystical experience (a view based on Isa. 6.1-4) in a context where Moses is cited as saying about the deity that 'no man shall see my face and live' (Exod. 33.20b). The author of the Ascension of Isaiah assumes that Isaiah did see God and he gives the prophet's vision a Christian interpretation. This by implication criticizes Exod. 33.20b, and indeed everyone who appealed to Moses to deny the possibility of mystical revelation. The effect of this scriptural comparison is that the author preferred the citation of a prophetic text to that of the Torah. This goes against the principles of interpretation laid down in rabbinic literature, where the Torah takes precedence over other parts of the Hebrew Bible.

4.21-22 then mentions a list of inspired writings from the Bible but strikingly fails to include the Torah among them. In contrast to Paul, who explained that the Torah described appearances of the pre-existent Christ (1 Cor. 10.4), the author of the Ascension of Isaiah gives no sign that he believed this was so. This again suggests that he thought that the Torah had less value for the use of Christian scriptural exegetes than other parts of the Hebrew Bible. There is perhaps the hint here that Moses had never known the true God whom the Beloved One revealed, because of his use in contemporary Judaism

It is interesting to note that some of the later Gnostic literature adopts a still more radical attitude towards the Torah. An example of this is the Apocryphon of John, in which more than once the Saviour is made to say that the creation of the world did not happen 'as Moses said'. While a comparison with Gnosticism should not be pressed, the Ascension of Isaiah evidently came from an author whose outlook on the world, which stemmed from his conviction of belonging to a marginalized group, meant that he repudiated other people's religious beliefs as the Gnostics would later do. He was probably suspicious of the Torah because of its use by the Jews, but his own Jewish heritage led him to see the second two divisions of the Hebrew Bible, the Writings and the Prophets, as valuable predictions of Christ. The Ascension of Isaiah thus by implication denies the basis of authority which undergirded Jewish religious belief and it possibly represents a stage towards the Gnostic suspicion of Moses; but its author never explicitly says that Moses was wrong or uninspired, so that sensitive interpretation is needed of this issue.

The author's hostility towards Judaism must be seen in the context of Jewish–Christian relations in the early Common Era. Such a comparison shows that his view was far from exceptional and it must not be exaggerated for that reason. Relations between the two religions had been problematic from the ministry of Jesus onwards. Jesus conflicted with some Jews over his attitude towards the Temple in

Jerusalem. Jewish hostility to Christians began at an early date, typified by the case of Saul who persecuted the church in the manner described by Acts 8.1-3. Acts takes pains to stress Jewish malevolence in the conflicts prompted by Christian preaching which occurred throughout the Mediterranean world (e.g. Acts 17.5). A prominent reason for Jewish hostility was the fact that Christians preached as messiah someone who had been crucified by the Romans when the Torah said that those whose bodies were exhibited on a gibbet were cursed by God (Deut. 21.22-23; see also Gal. 3.13). A further cause of tension was the Christian belief that Jesus was divine. This added to the offence of preaching a crucified messiah by asserting that there was a 'Lord' as well as a 'God' in heaven (cf. 1 Cor. 8.6) which represented a widening of the monotheistic concept.

Christians responded to this hostility by criticizing the Jews for their rejection of the messiah and by suggesting their complicity in his death. To this was added after 70 CE, and more particularly after 135 CE, the belief that the destruction of Jerusalem was a divine punishment for their behaviour. Paul makes a strong criticism of Judaism in one of his earliest letters, 1 Thess. 2.14-16, where he says that the Jews had killed the Lord Jesus and the prophets, were heedless of the divine will, and subject to retribution as a consequence. Mt. 27.25 shows that such feelings persisted after the fall of Jerusalem (cf Lk 19:43-44, 21:20-24) (70 CE) when the Gospel-writer makes the crowd tell Pilate that the blood of Jesus would be upon them and on their children. This view of Judaism is present in an even stronger form in Jn 19.1-16, which was written in the late first century CE, where the Jewish authorities are presented as actively persuading Pilate to crucify Jesus. A variety of second- and third-century Christian literature reflected on the divine purpose in the failure of the Second Jewish Revolt (132–135 CE) (see e.g. Justin, *Dial.* 110; *1 Apol.* 47; Origen, *Contra Celsum* 1.47; Hippolytus, *Dem. adv. Jud.* 6-7). The Ascension of Isaiah is one of the earliest sources to offer a Christian comment on the destruction of Jerusalem (cf. Lk. 19.43-44; 21.20-24).

This material that is critical of Judaism, although part of the Ascension of Isaiah, lies outside the historical review. This creates the impression that relations with Jews did not form part of the immediate crisis which the apocalypse was written to address. The heart of the problem is revealed by the First Vision, in which the author mentions his dislike of fellow Christians (3.21-31) and of the Roman government (4.1-13). That evidence must now be examined.

Problems in the Second-century Church

Two distinct groups are criticized in the First Vision: the 'wicked shepherds and elders' (3.24) and the Romans, the latter symbolized by the figure of Beliar who appeared as Nero (4.1-13). Although the identity of the second group is perhaps easier to surmise than that of the first, the fact that 'shepherd' was a traditional term in Jewish literature for leaders (see Ezek. 34; 1 En. 89.68), while 'elder' was a technical term for the same in Judaism and early Christianity (see 3 Jn 1), indicates that the author's difficulty lay especially with the church leaders in the second-century Christian body. The identity of these 'wicked shepherds and elders' is not stated but the impression offered is that the author disliked the behaviour of church leaders in general rather than that of a specific group of leaders in a particular place. These are said to be greedy, ambitious people who vied for office when their behaviour showed that they were unworthy to hold it.

The basis of the author's complaint against other Christians can be ascertained from several hints which he offers in this section. 3.21 says that the majority of Christians had turned aside from the apostles' 'teaching...faith...love...and purity'. This amounts to the admission that Christianity in the second century had lost much of its initial *élan*. The author states further that the Holy Spirit had withdrawn from many (3.26b) and he says that this was because of 'the spirit of error and of fornication, and of vainglory, and of the love of money among those who are said to be servants of that One' (3.27-28). This 'withdrawal of the Holy Spirit' implies a cessation of apocalyptic activity. The climax of the section (3.31) says that more powerful people had 'made ineffective the prophecies of the prophets who were before me...and my visions also'. While this statement is difficult to interpret, the view taken in this Guide is that it represents the author's own complaint about opposition from the leaders and that the pseudepigraphy briefly recedes at this point to permit a personal comment. This view is based on what appears to be the likelihood that 3.21-31, the author's description of the post-apostolic church, reflects something of his own experience of church life at the time.

The author's complaint against the leaders is bound up with what he took to be the withdrawal of the Holy Spirit from the church (3.26), and specifically with the attempt made by church leaders to silence prophetic oracles (3.31). The issue was one in which the status of prophecy featured prominently. Material in other parts of the apocalypse confirms that this was so. 2.7-11 presents the prophets as an isolated group who were spurned by their co-religionists but who continued to practise apocalyptic activity 6.14, 17 excludes all but the prophets from the place where Isaiah's ascension took place as if the revelation were felt to apply only to a small circle of recognized prophets. 2.7-11 and 3.21-31 come close to saying that the prophets alone guarded the Christian tradition in the second century. This implies that the Ascension of Isaiah was written for a prophetic circle, or at least a circle that valued prophecy and doubtless included prophets, at a time when the rise of institutional leadership was undermining the respect in which the prophets were held.

The kind of prophecy disputed in this way is illustrated by the two apocalyptic visions included in the Ascension of Isaiah. The First Vision is an eschatological prophecy which anticipates that the Beloved would soon return to introduce his earthly kingdom. It has a prognostic element (4.14-18) and the fact that the material is called 'a vision' (3.31; 4.20) probably implies that it was received or confirmed by apocalyptic revelation. That the church leaders are very obviously criticized here (3.21-31), and in much the same terms as the Roman government (4.1-13), provides a natural explanation of why the circle in question should have been opposed by the leaders if their views had become widely known. This was because they had possibly said that the church leaders were allied to Beliar and so that they were not true disciples of the Beloved One.

The Second Vision confirms that the author's understanding of prophecy had a prominent mystical aspect. It was bound up with the phenomenon of visionary ascension to heaven. Mystical ascension was a familiar feature of late Jewish apocalyptic as we know from a variety of writings associated with figures such as Enoch, Abraham and Moses (see the description of these in Gruenwald 1980: 29-72). As with Asc. Isa. 3.21-31 there are reasons for supposing that chs. 6–11 draw on aspects of the author's own experience. The introduction to the Vision in chapter 6 describes how a group of disciples gathered around the mystic as he made his ascension, and the cosmology has clearly been constructed with Trinitarian considerations in view. This Christian orientation of the material suggests that it too represents the kind of prophetic activity which the author undertook and over which he conflicted with the church leaders.

Asc. Isa. 3.21-31 thus describes what is essentially a dispute about authority. It shows the author's conviction that his friends had the right to proclaim divine truth because they had learned the heavenly secrets through mystical revelation. He argued that this was a direct continuation of the model of authority which had existed in first-century Christianity (3.21). This claim was apparently resisted by others who believed that the grounds of authority now rested with the ministerial orders which had emerged by the second century CE. This indicates a dispute between charismatic and institutional authority in early second-century Christianity. The author's view of the demise of prophecy is revealed here and it involves the assertion that most Christians no longer followed apostolic ways.

What the 'wicked shepherds and elders' might have said about this situation can be ascertained from the letters of Ignatius. Ignatius leaves little doubt about where he thought that authority resided. He says in Eph. 6.1 that 'one must regard the bishop as the Lord himself'; Magn. 6.1 adds to this the fact that 'the bishop is set over you in the place of God...the presbyters are in the place of the council of the apostles... and the deacons are entrusted with the service of Jesus Christ'. These comments affirm a hierarchy of ministry in which the bishop was owed the same respect that Christians offered to God and where the presbyters and deacons exercised a delegated and subordinate authority.

In the light especially of 3.31 it seems that the author of the Ascension of Isaiah felt that his position as a visionary prophet had been threatened by claims such as this made by the institutional leaders, who were doubtless trying to silence rival claimants to authority through their appeal to the ministerial offices. He reacted by writing an apocalypse in which the behaviour of these officials was censured (in the same terms that the Jews and the Romans were criticized) and in which the validity of apocalyptic activity was affirmed.

The Ascension of Isaiah and the Demise of Prophecy

In the light of this discussion it is helpful to set the evidence of the Ascension of Isaiah within the context of the development, and ultimate demise, of prophecy in early Christianity. Such a discussion must begin with Judaism. It has sometimes been argued that prophecy had all but died out in Judaism before the Christian period (this is done on the basis of a passage such as *b. Yom.* 9b). While there is evidence to suggest that at times prophets were unavailable (1 Macc. 4.46 is an example of this) this theory must not be held universally true, since we know from sources such as 1QpHab 7.1-5 and Philo, *Rer. Div. Her.*

259 that the prophetic spirit was believed to be active in at least some sectors of Judaism at the time. The development of an apocalyptic interest in Judaism from the second century BCE confirms that it was thought possible to achieve a more direct contact with God than exegesis of the Hebrew Bible allowed.

There seem to have been three different types of prophets in primitive Christianity. These were wandering prophets, church prophets confined to a particular community, and ordinary church members as they exercised a prophetic gift. There was doubtless an overlap between these different categories. The substratum of Matthew and Luke called Q (albeit a hypothetical source) contains material addressed to wandering prophets. An example of this is Mt. 8.20, the saying that foxes had holes and the birds a nest but that the Son of Man had nowhere to lay his head (see also Lk. 10.8-12). The wandering prophet's lifestyle is further described by the Didache, a Syrian Christian text written in the late first century CE. The Didache retains a high view of the prophets but by implication acknowledges that they were decreasing in numbers. According to Did. 10.7 prophets could give thanks in a free form of prayer but other people must follow a set form. 11.7 forbids readers to reprove any prophet who spoke by the Spirit on the grounds that this was an unforgivable sin. Chapter 13 states that every true prophet deserved support (13.1), as did the true teacher (13.2), but that this was not the case for false prophets, rules for whose discernment are found in ch. 11. These rules included the observation of how a prophet behaved: those who asked for money or stayed for more than a short period proved themselves to be false prophets. The firstfruits of produce were reserved for the prophets on the grounds that they were Christian High Priests (13.3). Only in the absence of prophets was such food to be given to the poor (13.4). This last reference shows the respect that the prophets enjoyed in the late first century but it acknowledges that they were not found in every community, otherwise the qualification would be meaningless (a point made by Friedrich 1983: 859).

The second type of prophet (a recognized class of person with considerable authority and attached to a particular church) is revealed by Acts 11.27-28 and 1 Cor. 12.28. The first of these passages describes how a person called Agabus travelled from Jerusalem to Antioch and predicted the famine which also prompted Paul's collection. The likelihood is that this was a special journey, possibly a regular exchange of prophets, between important churches. Agabus seems to have been a settled figure rather than a wandering charismatic. This view of 'the prophets' as a recognized class is supported by 1 Cor. 12.28 which mentions 'prophets' as second in importance to the apostles. It seems unlikely that Paul means by this 'all Christians inasmuch as they exercised a prophetic ministry'. His phrase 'first apostles and then prophets' denotes a special class of people whose prophetic gifts were regarded as exceptional.

1 Corinthians also discloses that every church member was regarded as exercising a prophetic ministry (1 Cor. 12–14). The issue which prompted this part of Paul's letter was apparently the fact that some in the community had begun to boast that their spiritual gifts were superior to others'. Paul addressed this problem by using the image of the body in which each individual part was encouraged to work for the good of the whole. Paul says that he wanted all members of the church to prophesy (14.1-5), in a context in which prophecy is preferred for its intelligibility to the gift of tongues, which was an ecstatic language and consequently unintelligible until someone offered an interpretation. Women could prophesy as well as men (1 Cor. 11.5) despite Paul's view of female subordination to the male expressed in 1 Cor. 11.5-10. Prophetic experience among ordinary church members was one of the hallmarks of first-century Christianity. What qualified a person to be 'a prophet' in the exceptional sense rather than simply 'to prophesy' as described here is not certain, but community recognition of a person's gift (and perhaps apostolic validation) was no doubt an important factor. 'Prophets' as a class of people enjoyed great authority in those early days, as 1 Cor. 12.28 shows.

It has been argued by Pesce (1983) that the Ascension of Isaiah originated among a circle of wandering prophets. An alternative expression of this view, proposed by Hall (1990), holds that the text was written for prophets who gathered periodically from different communities to experience apocalyptic revelation. Hall believes that the Ascension of Isaiah was written to persuade a recalcitrant church of the need for belief in the Beloved One's descent and ascension. The view taken in this Guide is that the apocalypse was concerned more especially with resisting Roman hostility as expressed by the sacrifice test and that the distinction between different kinds of Christians in 3.21-31 shows a subsidiary but important cause of discontent in the author's mind. Nevertheless, the theory that the first readers of the apocalypse were wandering prophets is an attractive one, especially when we consider that passages such as Asc. Isa. 4.13 and 5.13

apparently advocate a displaced lifestyle.

The Ascension of Isaiah certainly reveals a very different situation from that found in first-century Corinth. In contrast to 1 Cor. 14.1-5, where Paul said that every Christian could expect to prophesy, the author of the Ascension of Isaiah complains that the Holy Spirit had been withdrawn from 'many' (3.26) and that prophetic oracles were even opposed by influential people (3.31). He includes a narrative which presents the prophets as marginalized figures (2.7-11) and which carefully chooses those judged worthy to witness Isaiah's ascension (6.14; 17). Both the numbers of people who exercised a prophetic ministry and the status of prophecy itself are quite different in the two writings, and it is evident that attitudes had changed in the period between which they were written. The apocalypse give the impression that 'prophecy' was no longer practised by every Christian and that 'the prophets' in the second of the senses mentioned here were now being displaced by the 'shepherds and elders'. It should be noticed that institutional leaders had not featured in the hierarchy of authority which Paul had mentioned in 1 Cor. 12.28.

This change in attitudes to prophecy can be illustrated from other Christian literature. Ephesians, which is almost certainly a pseudonymous text speaks of the church as 'built on the foundation of the apostles and prophets' (2.20) as if the influence of prophets, like that of the apostles, lay in the past when it was written (c. 80–90 CE). With this should be compared some further evidence from the Didache. Did. 15.1 says that bishops and deacons must be respected as approved by the Lord and that they 'fulfilled the ministry of the prophets' in Christian churches. They must not be slighted but deserved the same respect as the prophets and teachers. This comment finds its meaning in a situation in which the leaders were being ignored and the prophets held in great respect. The Didache evidently comes from a time of change when the need for institutional leadership had been recognized and when such leaders were emerging, but when people were also more inclined to listen to prophets, so that the leaders struggled to gain respect.

The emergence of institutional leadership in the late first century CE is revealed by other writings too. 1 Clem. 42 states that the apostles had received the Gospel from Jesus and that they appointed the firstfruits of their converts to be bishops and deacons. 1 Clem. 44 states that the apostles foresaw strife over the bishop's office and that they created a 'succession' in which 'other approved men' succeeded to the position on the death of the office-holder. Ignatius also lays great emphasis on the threefold hierarchy of ministerial orders in the church, as mentioned already in this chapter, and he saw there a reflection of the purpose and authority of God.

Although the evidence is sparse it does seem that some Christians opposed apocalyptic experience in the period immediately before the Ascension of Isaiah was written. The author of Jn 3.13, whose work achieved its present form c. 100 CE, denied that anyone had ascended to heaven except the Son of Man who had descended from heaven. This verse seems set against Jewish claims about mystical revelation but it criticizes Christian apocalypticism as well. This was because of the Fourth Evangelist's belief that Jesus had fully revealed the Father which made mystical ascension unnecessary. It is noteworthy that the author of the Ascension of Isaiah apparently agreed with John's view that Jesus had achieved everything needed for salvation but he retained the practice of heavenly ascension.

This information helps to explain the situation of the prophets revealed by the Ascension of Isaiah. The apocalypse indicates that, in contrast to the earlier situation, the prophets had become marginalized figures in the second century, and ch. 6 implies that they banded together for support. This obsolescence of the prophets can be traced back to the beginnings in the first century, when the Didache and shows that prophets were becoming less easy to find. This text confirms that prophets were no longer present in every community but it differs markedly from the Ascension of Isaiah in terms of the respect in which those who remained were held. The Ascension of Isaiah in many ways represents the complete opposite of the situation revealed by the Didache in its author's claim that prophets were now ignored and even repressed while the leaders held office and were opposed only by each other. He says that prophets were now found only in 'scattered places' (3.28) and hints that they must come together to find support (2.7-11; cf. ch. 6). The author of the Ascension of Isaiah evidently saw himself as a member of an obsolescent group—'the prophets'—who had once enjoyed an authority in the church second only to the apostles. Comparison between the Didache and the Ascension of Isaiah demontrates the status of prophecy in different stages of decline. This situation anticipates the final death of mystical prophecy with the rejection of the Montanist movement in the later second century (c. 175 CE).

Asc. Isa. 3.21-31 thus addressed a situation in which the author found his position as a prophet and his visions of the heavenly world rejected by the more powerful church leaders. This situation caused him concern, but this was not the immediate reason why the apocalypse was written. To find what that reason was we must turn to ch. 4 and examine the grounds of the author's dislike of the Romans.

Roman Attitudes to Christians

At the beginning of ch. 4 the author moves from a description of life in the church (3.21-31) to a more pressing concern. This was the problem of relations with the Roman government (4.1-13). The view taken in this Guide is that the author had become aware of the new development that is described in Pliny's letter to Trajan and produced his apocalypse as a response to that situation. The Ascension of Isaiah compares the imposition of the sacrifice test with Nero's persecution of the Christians in 64 CE and warns that the Christians were in danger of death if they refused to comply with the demand to worship Beliar (the point made by ch. 5). This hypothesis why the Roman government is presented in the apocalypse as embodying demonic forces, symbolized by the Beliar mythology, and it also accounts for the language used there about 'sacrifice' (4.8) and 'images' (4.11).

The situation addressed by the Ascension of Isaiah looks back on a history of difficult relations between the Christians and the Romans. The Christians first appeared to the Romans as a sect of the Jews. The book of Acts states that Paul had had an opportunity to defend his faith in Jesus before Roman officials (ch. 24 onwards) but this is not to say that the Romans were able to distinguish Christians from Jews in these early years. The most distinctive feature of the Christian position, it must have seemed to them, was that Christians claimed as messiah and Lord someone who had been put to death by a provincial official in the very recent past. Apart from this the Christians would have seemed very similar to the Jews in Roman eyes. The Jews were a well-known group but they were regarded as eccentric in the ancient world. This was because they circumcised their sons, refused to eat pork, and stubbornly retained a monotheistic belief. On the other hand they enjoyed an established religious tradition and many Romans admired their ethical code. For this reason Jews were generally allowed their religious freedom in Roman cities. Such protection was made official by Julius Caesar in an edict that was later reaffirmed by Augustus. This left Jews free to conduct synagogue worship and to send their Temple taxes to

Jerusalem. Even the First Revolt (66–70 CE) did not result in the removal of this privileged status, except that Jews were thereafter required to pay the former Temple levy to the pagan god Jupiter Capitolinus.

Romans thus tolerated Jewish people but made no pretence of understanding them. Roman religion was essentially pantheistic and bound up with reverence for a variety of deities which tended to increase in number as time wore on (see MacMullen 1981: 1-18). The Romans reacted to foreign cults, especially eastern ones, by subsuming them under more familiar names and rituals (see for instance what is said about Barnabas and Paul in Acts 14.12). Monotheism remained a difficult concept for Romans, as it did for many other people. Even Platonic philosophy, with which Jewish mysticism had certain points of contact, believed in 'the gods' rather than 'God' and to this extent supported the pantheon of popular mythology. Monotheists could easily pass as atheists in the ancient world on the grounds that, although they paid due homage to their own god, they refused to honour anybody else's. This was felt to have dangerous consequences by a superstitious Roman populace, as if a lack of respect for all the gods might bring retribution on the whole community from those deities who held themselves to have been spurned in this way. Jews were consequently held in some degree of suspicion but generally also tolerated in most cities of the empire.

The Christians were known to be Jewish sectarians but they were almost everywhere disowned by the Jews and they had no long-established precedent to protect them as their religion separated from Judaism. It is in the context of Jewish agitation that Christians first come to notice in Roman literature. Suetonius reports that Claudius expelled the Jews from Rome (in 49 CE) because of disturbances made there 'at the instigation of Chrestus' (*Claudius*, 25.4). 'Chrestus' is probably a corrupt form of 'Christ(us)'. A plausible interpretation of this passage is that it alludes to Jewish-Christian disturbances in Rome—disturbances about Christ—at a time even before the New Testament documents were written. We do not know how many Jews were expelled on that occasion. It may have been little more than a token gesture, for Jewish and Christian communities still remained in Rome (see Jeffers 1991: chapter 1). But tensions within the Jewish community had come to imperial attention barely twenty years after the death of Jesus. This illustrates the background to the later experience of conflict between the Christians and the Romans.

Fifteen years later there occurred the infamous persecution under Nero. Tacitus (*Annals* 15.44, 2-8) says that Nero fastened on, tortured and murdered 'a class hated for their abominations', that is the Christians. He did this to scotch the rumour that he himself had ordered the fire which destroyed a large part of Rome. We do not know how many Christians perished as a result of Nero's actions but the numbers were probably not inconsiderable (see 1 Clem. 6.1-2). 1 Clem. 5.4, followed by Ign., *Rom.* 4.3 and Asc. Isa. 4.3, implies that Peter perished in the pogrom. So great was the humiliation of the Christians, Tacitus says, that a feeling of compassion arose in the city even for those who were regarded as criminals at the severity of their punishment. A crucial element in this report is the statement that Christians were popularly suspected of committing 'abominations'. This suspicion recurs in the correspondence between Pliny and Trajan where Pliny acknowledges that those who were tortured confirmed only the innocuous nature of Christian religious practices, rather to his surprise. That Christians were popularly suspected of malpractice is confirmed also by Suetonius (*Nero*, 16.2) who describes Christianity as a 'new and wicked superstition'. It seems that Christians were generally held to display suspicious behaviour in Roman eyes, probably because of their secret meetings and the nature of their eucharistic practices.

This pagan judgment on Christianity, however unfair and misinformed it was, at least shows the extent to which the new religion had spread in a short space of time. Tacitus's report about the Neronian Persecution demonstrates a growing Roman perception of Christians as *Christians* rather than as Jews, and this seems to differ from the attitude of Claudius who dealt with the problem of Jewish–Christian agitation (if this is a correct interpretation of the incident) by expelling people called *Jews* from Rome, although that group may have included Christians. By Nero's time Christians were known as Christians, and thus as a religious group distinct from the Jews, and they had acquired an unfavourable reputation.

For all their severity Nero's actions look more like an an attempt to find a convenient scapegoat than what could be called an organized persecution. Indeed, there seems to have been no organized persecution of Christians before that instigated by the emperor Decius in the third century, merely a series of sporadic actions against them (see De Ste Croix 1963: 6-7). Thus it is disputed whether there was a 'persecution' in this sense under Domitian in the last decade of the first century CE. Dio Cassius (*Epitome* 67.14) says that a charge of 'atheism' was brought against Flavius Clemens and Flavia Domitilla at that time and that 'many others who made shipwreck on Jewish customs' were condemned and some of them executed. This report, however, is ambiguous and it might be taken to indicate that those who suffered in this way were, precisely, Jews and not Christians. Eusebius records another story, probably an apocryphal one, of how the grandsons of Jude were hauled before Domitian but dismissed (and not punished) when the emperor learned that the kingdom they were expecting was not of this world (*Hist. Eccl.*, 3.20), although Eusebius does say that Flavius Clemens and Flavia Domitilla were exiled to Pontia for their Christian beliefs. Frend notes the possibility that there were 'anti-Christian outbreaks in Asia following on natural disaster' around this period (1965: 212), but Collins points to the apologetic nature of patristic reports about this incident to suggest that those who suffered were again Jews (1984: 69). It is far from certain that Domitian persecuted Christians in a formal way, and by no means clear that the book of Revelation was written to deal with the experience of persecution at all (see Collins 1984). The Ascension of Isaiah, which was written in the reign of either Trajan or Hadrian, offers no evidence that Domitian persecuted Christians although it does mention the Neronian Persecution, and the silence of the apocalypse on this matter should perhaps be regarded as important evidence.

The correspondence between Pliny and Trajan (*Ep.* 10.96-97) suggests that a different situation had developed in the early second century CE (see De Ste Croix 1963: 9). This was one in which Christians were denounced (even anonymously) and punished just for being Christians. Pliny had apparently not met Christians before and told Trajan that he was uncertain of the grounds of their offence. He asked whether the Christians were to be punished for holding to the name of Christ alone or rather on suspicion that they had committed secret crimes associated with the name. No specific answer was provided to this question but Trajan was prepared to say that they must be punished if they refused to recant when required.

The sacrifice test was the crucial feature of this new situation. Pliny explains that he required Christians who were arraigned in this way to pray to the Roman gods, to offer incense before the imperial statue and statues of the gods, and to curse Christ. This was not so much an edict for emperor-worship as a demonstration of loyalty to the state in the reverence addressed to statues of Trajan and the gods. Pliny says that he had punished those who refused to do this for obstinacy. Trajan confirmed the value of the test but he did say that Christians must not be made the victims of anonymous accusation. The test which Pliny used derived from earlier Roman investigation of Jews and it had first been used in Antioch in 67 CE (see De Ste Croix 1963: 20; Frend 1965: 135-36). The new element in its use on this occasion was the requirement to curse Christ, which for Christians was tantamount to cursing God and something which Pliny says that pious Christians would refuse to do.

The reference to 'secret crimes' in Pliny's letter is puzzling but a possible explanation is suggested by Frend (1965: 221-22), who thinks that Pliny believed that Christians belonged to an illegal Jewish *collegium* or association. *Collegia* had acquired a bad name in Bithynia and Pliny had little hesitation in suppressing them. Common meals were the hallmark of such *collegia* as of course they were of early Christianity. The *collegium* theory may explain this reference in Pliny's letter and it may even supply the reason for the martyrdom of Ignatius. On this view the bishop was punished because he was known to be the titular head of the church in Antioch which was viewed in an unfavourable light by the authorities there.

The Ascension of Isaiah seems to reflect a knowledge of the sacrifice test. Much of chs. 4 and 5 of the apocalypse can be explained as a response to Roman hostility exhibited in this way. The Bithynian situation provides a natural explanation of the references to the Roman government as embodying demonic powers (4.4), making blasphemous demands (4.6), demanding sacrifice (4.8), and erecting the imperial statue in every city (4.11). We do not know whether the author's circle had suffered such investigation themselves or whether the author simply feared that they might do so. If the latter is true their status as religious pietists who refused to compromise with worldly demands (cf. 3.25) would probably have meant that they were the most likely people in the Christian body to suffer martyrdom. The Ascension of Isaiah establishes a link between prophecy and piety in several passages (e.g. 2.7-11) which implies that only those who were possessed by the Spirit like the author and his friends would remain faithful in this way.

The Ascension of Isaiah describes martyrdom as the final fate of those who resisted Beliar's demands, but the author does imply that this would be an isolated occurrence. He seems to indicate that the majority of the faithful would survive by adopting a displaced form of existence until the time of the divine intervention (2.7-11; 4.13; 5.13). We do not know how literally the author intended his material about the prophets' isolated lifestyle to be taken but it was probably a way of warning readers not to come too readily to Roman attention. The material advocating prudent withdrawal (esp. 5.13) is perhaps to be seen as a warning against the phenomenon of voluntary martyrdom through which some readers might have been tempted to emulate the death of Jesus (as Ignatius had done). The description of Isaiah's martyrdom in ch. 5 was apparently written with a knowledge of the death of Ignatius but it is difficult to know what significance the author attached to that event. The Ascension of Isaiah adopts a realistic attitude towards the likely outcome of any encounter with the Romans and for that reason suggests that caution was more prudent than rash encounter given the fact that the death penalty was in vogue.

It would be wrong to say that the Ascension of Isaiah is necessarily typical of the response which the Christians made to Roman sovereignty in the first hundred years of the new religion. Both Paul (in Rom. 13) and the author of 1 Pet. 2.13, 17 advocated respectful obedience to the authorities including the emperor. This reveals a willingness to accept the existing political situation, probably because both authors believed that the returning Christ would soon introduce a new kingdom in which different standards would pertain. The Ascension of Isaiah comes from a later period when a Roman governor had begun to punish Christians and determined their loyalty by a public test of belief. This was a very different situation to that found in the majority of the New Testament writings, and it produced the different response towards Rome which the Ascension of Isaiah represents.

The Purpose of the Ascension of Isaiah

This evidence indicates that the Ascension of Isaiah was written in a situation where its author had become uneasy with life in the post-apostolic church, and where the intolerant attitude of the Romans towards the Christians had caused a major crisis of confidence. Although apocalyptic literature was not addressed exclusively to crises, this apocalypse shows that a growing pessimism about life in general motivated the author. He saw this combination of circumstances as putting pressure on pious Christians and he responded, first by offering assurance that the Beloved One's kingdom would soon appear (4.14-18), and then by explaining that the Beloved had already defeated Beliar in what constitutes a more systematic explanation of salvation (chs. 6–11).

The First Vision embodies the hope for an imminent divine intervention through which the existing order would be transformed. Its eschatology has a strong future orientation. The author's interest in this section lies in contrasting the state of the present with the new situation which he expected to emerge at the parousia. The Ascension of Isaiah embodies a 'millenarian' hope, by which is meant that its author expected the returning Christ to establish an earthly kingdom from which Beliar and his hosts would be excluded and where the pious would enjoy a form of life that they had not experienced before. This kingdom would not be an end in itself but it was to be the prelude to a heavenly immortality when the human body would be shaken off to yield an incorporeal life in the heavenly world (4.17). Such millenarianism had been a prominent feature of earlier Christian eschatology (see Bietenhard 1953). The author of the Ascension of Isaiah confidently asserts that what had been promised in the past but not fulfilled would now shortly come to completion (4.14-18). His hope for the Beloved's earthly kingdom formed one of the ways in which this author encouraged his readers.

Much of what has been said so far concerns the First Vision but it would be wrong to exclude chs. 6–11 from consideration. The Second Vision lacks any formal expression of the *parousia* hope to match the eschatology of 4.14-18 but it does share a common purpose with the First Vision in terms of its provision of hope for a difficult situation. The main element in the Second Vision is Isaiah's vision of the Beloved's descent and ascent through which the power of Beliar was destroyed. This part of the Ascension of Isaiah shows the true nature of apocalyptic literature as concerned with the revelation of heavenly secrets. The Second Vision discloses information about the Beloved One and about salvation. The author offers an explanation of why life on earth was difficult, something that he connects with the behaviour of angels in the firmament (7.10) and with Beliar's earthly incarnation (ch. 4). He then offers an apocalyptic perspective on what the Beloved One had already achieved by drawing attention to the cross as the moment when these angels were 'judged and destroyed' (ch. 10), as Isaiah saw in his vision. The conclusion of the Ascension of Isaiah describes how the Beloved ascended to heaven and how the angels in the firmament worshipped him as he passed (11.23-33). Such offering of worship at the conclusion of the Vision is the author's apocalyptic demonstration that salvation had been provided, an assurance that is symbolized especially by the mediator's enthronement at the right hand of God (11.32). Readers were presented with this Vision as an item of 'transformative knowledge' which could change the way that they viewed their lives. They were encouraged to see Beliar, however powerful he was, as a defeated opponent and themselves as people who were supported by the Beloved One despite what was happening in the world around them.

The Second Vision thus differs from the First in offering a view of salvation in which spatial rather than temporal categories are used, so that the Ascension of Isaiah in its present form makes use of a *fusion* of these categories. The emphasis in chs. 6–11 falls on an apocalyptic interpretation of the atonement rather than on a prediction of future change. The author uses the seven-storied cosmology in these later chapters to describe what is effectively a situation at variance with reality. The truth about the readers' situation is revealed by the First Vision, in which they are portrayed as harassed by church authorities (3.31) and fearful of the Romans (4.1-13). The author's use of the cosmology, however, deliberately creates the impression that the opposite was the case. It makes God and the Beloved (and by implication those who worshipped them) supreme and Beliar less powerful than even the weakest angel in heaven through his place in the firmament. Both the arrangement of the cosmic system and the fact of the Beloved's victory are presented as items of revealed knowledge that were intended to work for the readers' benefit. By showing that God was in control and by denying the power of Beliar the author offered hope and encouragement which he intended to be read in conjunction with the millenarian hope found in the First Vision.

Further Reading

Relations between Jews and Christians
Relations between Jews and Christians in the early Common Era are examined by Gager (1983). All the books on the history of early Christianity mentioned in the Further Reading to Chapter 1 include discussion of this issue; see e.g. Chadwick 1967: 9-23. The significance of the destruction of Jerusalem for Christian writers is examined by Lampe (1984: 153-71), who notes that 135 CE tended to exercise the greater effect on the Christian imagination.

Prophecy in early Christianity
The history and significance of prophecy in early Christianity are explored by Hill (1979) and Aune (1983). There is also a valuable article on prophets in the early church by G. Friedrich in *TDNT* VI: 856-61.

Relations between Christians and Romans
In addition to the literature mentioned in the text of this Guide see Markus 1974: 24-47, and MacMullen 1984: 17-24. There is important material also in Thompson 1990, especially chapters 3 and 4 on the social and political setting of the book of Revelation.

3

A COMMENTARY ON THE ASCENSION OF ISAIAH

The Ascension of Isaiah contains valuable evidence for the history of second-century Christianity but it has often been ignored because of the difficulties surrounding its interpretation. This Guide now proceeds to offer a commentary on the apocalypse in the belief that that is the best way to explain its complex textual allusions and problems. The Ascension of Isaiah must be seen as a representative of post-apostolic Christianity in company with texts such as 1 Clement, Barnabas and the letters of Ignatius. Only by taking account of all the available evidence, including that provided by neglected literature, can scholarship hope to gain an accurate picture of the period under discussion.

Hezekiah, Manasseh and Isaiah

The Ascension of Isaiah opens with some narrative traditions about Isaiah. The author states that Hezekiah summoned Manasseh into his presence in his 'twenty-sixth' regnal year (1.1). This raises a problem of chronology because the Second Vision, which begins in 6.1, is set some six years earlier in the 'twentieth' year of Hezekiah's reign. The apocalypse makes no reference to the tradition of Manasseh's co-regency during Hezekiah's sickness which some scholars have posited to reconcile problems in the biblical chronology (see Thiele 1983: 64, 174-180).

Hezekiah summoned Manasseh into his presence with Isaiah and his son Josab as witnesses (1.2; for the need for two witnesses see Deut. 19.15). Isaiah is called a 'prophet' (a title which the Ascension of Isaiah understands in terms of apocalyptic revelation). Josab is the Shear-jashub mentioned by Isa. 7.3. The purpose of the meeting was for Hezekiah to hand to Manasseh 'the words of righteousness which the king himself had seen'. Later in 6.3 Isaiah is said to speak with Hezekiah 'the words of faith and righteousness', and Samnas and Jehoiakim are said to be 'doers of righteousness' in 6.17. 'Words of righteousness' seems to be almost a technical term for apocalyptic revelation in the Ascension of Isaiah. It emphasizes the connection between prophetic activity and godly living which is made throughout the apocalypse (see 2.7-11; esp. 2.9).

The description of Hezekiah's vision anticipates both the Visions found later in the apocalypse. 1.3 states that it concerned 'the eternal judgments, and the torments of Gehenna, and the prince of this world, and his angels and his authorities, and his powers' (1.3). 'The Prince of this World' is a title for Beliar, whom the apocalypse also calls Sammael, Beliar, Malkira and Matanbukus. These different titles all identify a single figure (see Knibb 1985: 151-52): the demon in the firmament whom ch. 4 says became associated with Nero. The Ascension of Isaiah shares with John (12.31; 14.30; 16.11) and with Paul (2 Cor. 4.4) the belief that the 'ruler of this world' was an inferior power who exercised control over human beings (see 7.9-12). Hezekiah's warning anticipates the destruction of Beliar which is described in different ways by 4.14 and 10.6-17.

1.3 contains a strong indication that the author was familiar with 1 Pet. 3.22. The phrase 'angels, authorities, powers' recalls the general New Testament conviction that Jesus' life and death had defeated Satan, but the form of language used here, despite its similarity to Pauline passages (e.g. Col. 2.15), finds an exact parallel only in 1 Pet. 3.22. Asc. Isa. 11.23-33 also suggests that the author knew that passage, from which he evidently derived the notion of the Beloved's heavenly ascension, his victory over the angels and enthronement at the right hand of God. This indicates that the apocalypse draws on a knowledge of the New Testament as well as of the Old Testament writings, a point which has not always been recognized in research. The Ascension of Isaiah is thus one of the earliest Christian texts to use the New Testament literature. The author's interest in the Beloved One's activity determines the way in which such material is used in the apocalypse (cf. 4.21-22).

The effect of this opening scene is to draw a sharp distinction between the characters of the two kings described. A number of themes coalesce here. Hezekiah is presented as a pious king who did

3. A Commentary on the Ascension of Isaiah 49

good deeds and who was reported to have enjoyed apocalyptic experience. This develops the suggestion of 2 Kings 18–20 and Isaiah 38 that he was a pious king who listened to the prophets. Manasseh by contrast proved to be a wicked king. He worked abominations (ch. 2) and persecuted the prophets (chs. 3 and 5). This contrast between good and evil, and support and repression of the prophets, illustrates the dualism which is a prominent feature of the Ascension of Isaiah (see below).

In 1.4 the christological title 'Beloved One' is used for the first time. This title was used for the king in pre-Christian Judaism (the superscription to Psalm 45 in the Septuagintal version, 'a song about the Beloved One', makes this clear). The Beloved One in the Ascension of Isaiah is a divine being who shares the worship of God (7.17) and is subordinate only to God in the whole cosmic system. He is what might loosely be called 'the heavenly Christ' and he appears on earth as Jesus after his descent through the heavens (3.13-18; 11.2-22). The title reflects the mediator's unequalled status in the seventh heaven but it also retains the common early Christian conviction that Christ was subordinate to the Father (cf. 1 Cor. 8.6; 15.24-25). It may have been introduced to address Pliny's point that persecution was undertaken 'for the name' of Christ and thus to represent a response to this situation which reflected pious Christians' love for their Saviour.

Isaiah predicted that Hezekiah's warning would have no effect on Manasseh (1.7) and that he himself would be killed by the new king. 1.8 states that Beliar would dwell in Manasseh and that he would 'cause many in Jerusalem and Judah to desert the true faith'; Isaiah's death by sawing asunder is predicted as well (1.9). Hezekiah lamented this prophecy (1.10) but Isaiah said that Sammael's plan could not be thwarted (1.11). The statement that Isaiah would 'inherit the inheritance of the Beloved', which he makes about himself in 1.13, refers to his impending martyrdom, which is presented in the apocalypse as the outcome of the prophet's refusal to obey Beliar's demands (see ch. 5).

Chapter 2 describes Manasseh's reign. Manasseh abandoned his ancestral religion and served 'Satan, and his angels, and his powers' (2.2). The apocalypse contains a prominent dualism which has both a cosmological and an ethical aspect ('dualism' denotes the belief that there are two opposing forces at work in the world, of good and of evil). The cosmology draws a distinction between the heavens and the firmament and their respective occupants. The author explains that Beliar was excluded from the heavens and confined to the firmament. This was part of the saving knowledge which he wished to communicate to his readers. It reminded them of the insignificance of the Romans' authority despite the power which they exercised at this time. Beliar's position in the firmament contrasts strikingly with that of the three divine beings who sat enthroned in the seventh heaven (11.32-33). Such cosmological dualism is a way of denying Beliar's authority despite the fact that the demon was manifestly able to exercise power in the actions of the Roman government.

The Ascension of Isaiah also has an ethical dualism. By this is meant that it allows for only two kinds of behaviour which are typified respectively by Isaiah and by Manasseh. A person's behaviour is held to be a reflection of which heavenly power he or she worshipped. The faithful prophets preserved their religious practices and did good deeds. It is implied that these were a minority when the apocalypse was written (cf. 3.21; 4.9; 4.13). Those who had been deceived by Beliar acted arrogantly and persecuted the prophets. Manasseh is an example of this. In 2.3-4 the new king is said to have turned his father's house away from 'the words of wisdom and the service of the Lord' to serve Beliar.

The result of this apostasy was that Manasseh committed a variety of lawless actions. The author says that Beliar strengthened Manasseh in causing apostasy and in the iniquity disseminated in Jerusalem (2.4). A catalogue of vices is mentioned including sorcery and magic, augury and divination, fornication and adultery, and the persecution of the righteous through different people, among whom is Belchira who reappears as Isaiah's accuser in ch. 3. The first four of these are crimes associated with foreign nations by Deut. 18.10-11. Such criticism is here significantly applied to the household of the Judaean king.

The Formation of the Wilderness Community

Isaiah was distressed at this lawlessness and the 'service of Satan' permitted in Jerusalem and he withdrew to Bethlehem (2.7). There too he found 'great iniquity'; he withdrew from Bethlehem and 'dwelt on a mountain in a desert place' (2.8). He was joined there by other prophets to form a wilderness community. The names of some of these prophets are given; Micah, old Ananias, Joel, Habakkuk, Josab (but the list is not historically accurate). The community is said to have been distinguished by its belief in the 'ascension into heaven' (2.9), a statement which reveals much about the nature of prophecy as the author understood it. These prophets were 'clothed in sackcloth' (a traditional

3. A Commentary on the Ascension of Isaiah

Old Testament sign of mourning); 'all of them were prophets' (a significant statement in view of what the author says about the demise of prophecy in 3.21-31); 'they had nothing with them, but were destitute and they all lamented bitterly over the going astray of Israel' (2.10).

The community described here evidently had a strong penitential function and this may show something of how the author and his friends understood their position in the church. The Qumran sect saw itself in a similar light but nothing of substance connects the Ascension of Isaiah with that circle. The author states that these prophets 'had nothing to eat except wild herbs, [which] they gathered from the mountain' (2.11). This suggests an ascetic tendency but it probably has mystical significance as well. The eating of herbs was regarded as preparatory for apocalyptic experience in Judaism (see 4 Ezra 9.26; 12.51; cf. Dan. 10.2-3) and in other religious traditions. It seems likely that this diet was intended to induce the kind of experience which the Second Vision records. The prophets remained on the mountain, the passage concludes, for 'two years of days' (2.11).

2.12 reintroduces Belchira but there are considerable textual problems in 2.12-16. Belchira's uncle Zedekiah had been the teacher of the four hundred prophets of Baal in the reign of Ahab (2.12). Zedekiah's harsh treatment of Micaiah-ben-Imlah is mentioned in 2.12-13. The analogy is carefully chosen for Micaiah, like Isaiah, had seen a vision of the Lord (the experience recorded in 1 Kgs 22.19). Zedekiah is said to have struck Micaiah on the cheek (2.12, based on 1 Kgs 22.24); the victim was thrown into prison with Zedekiah the prophet (2.13) but this reference finds no support in the biblical narrative. 2.14-16 are obscure and difficult to interpret. In 2.14 Elijah is said to have 'reproved Ahaziah and Samaria' and prophesied that 'he would die on his bed of sickness'; this is an allusion to the death of Ahaziah in 2 Kings 1. Elijah also predicted the destruction of Samaria by Shalmaneser in 722 BCE (2.14). When the false prophets with Ahaziah heard this they persuaded the king to kill Micaiah. This section may be difficult to follow but it well suits its context in the Ascension of Isaiah. Micaiah's death at the hands of a lawless king foreshadows that of Isaiah who perished in the same way. Both had seen the seated deity, the vision for which Isaiah met his death in ch. 5. Micaiah thus foreshadows Isaiah in his martyrdom as well as his mysticism.

Isaiah is Accused and Arrested

Belchira discovered and visited the prophets in their wilderness retreat (3.1). This incident has been linked, almost certainly wrongly, with the appearance of the so-called Wicked Priest at Qumran when the community was celebrating a festival (see Flusser 1953). The result of this visitation was that Belchira accused Isaiah of various crimes before Mannaseh. 3.6-12 describes three charges which he laid against the prophet in this way. He said that Isaiah and the others had prophesied treasonably against Jerusalem and the cities of Judah, and had predicted that these would be destroyed and that the king would be taken captive (3.6). This alludes to the fate of Manasseh recorded in 2 Chron. 33.11 (but not in the books of Kings), and it also hints that the destruction of Jerusalem in 70 CE fell within the divine will. The comment that 'they prophesy, lies against Israel and Judah' (3.7) has a deep irony in the light of 70 CE and serves to authenticate Isaiah's prophecy, which was evidently constructed with an eye to what had happened on that occasion.

The second charge (3.8-10) reports that Isaiah claimed, 'I see more than Moses the prophet'. Belchira then cites the second half of Exod. 33.20, 'There is no man who can see the Lord and live', to prove that this statement was wrong. Isa. 6.1 is next paraphrased and set against the citation from Moses ('I have seen the LORD, and behold I am alive') as evidence for Belchira's assertion that Isaiah was a liar.

The Talmudic version of this dispute (*b. Yeb.* 49b) helps to explain the significance of this scriptural comparison. This passage sets Exod. 33.20b against Isa. 6.1 to assert that 'all the prophets looked into a dim glass, but Moses looked through a clear glass'. This comment evidently means that Moses was right in saying that God could not be seen and that the prophets had simply *imagined* that they had seen God in the relevant passages. The dispute as recorded in the Ascension of Isaiah takes a different view from the Talmud. The author of the apocalypse assumes that God *could* be seen and he gives this vision which Isaiah had received a Christian interpretation. This is evident in the two apocalyptic Visions. The First Vision, which follows the passage almost immediately in 3.13, describes the activity of the Beloved One as the divine subordinate in what is clearly a binitarian context. The Second Vision has a Trinitarian outlook and it concludes with a picture of the three divine beings enthroned in the seventh heaven (11.32-33). The implication of the Ascension of Isaiah is that Isaiah was right in his claim to have seen God, which implies that those who appealed to

Moses to deny the possibility of mystical vision and the value of Christian theology were misguided. This second charge has the effect of presenting Christianity as a religious revelation superior to Judaism and it contains the hint that Moses did not foresee the Beloved One at all.

The third charge is mentioned in 3.10. Isaiah is alleged to have called Jerusalem Sodom and its rulers the people of Gomorrah. This charge is based on Isa. 1.10 ('Hear the word of the Lord, you rulers of Sodom! Give ear to the teaching of our God, you people of Gomorrah!'). Sodom and Gomorrah were the cities destroyed by God in Genesis 19. Like 3.6 this reference seems to be an allusion to the events of 70 CE and it implies that Jerusalem had been doomed to destruction as a punishment by God. As mentioned earlier, this material in the apocalypse that is critical of Judaism should neither be ignored nor given an importance which neglects the evidence of other Christian literature that it has a conventional nature. Yet 3.8-10 (cf. 4.21-22) does by implication pour scorn on Moses and this point must be acknowledged as evidence for the history of relations between the Christians and the Jews in the early second century.

The author emphasizes Beliar's part in the charges laid against Isaiah (3.11). The prophet was arrested on the basis of what was said and brought before the king (3.12).

The First Vision

What this Guide calls the First Vision (3.13–4.22) now begins. The First Vision is a Christian eschatological prophecy. It takes the form of an apocalyptic historical review and identifies four periods between the Beloved One's appearance as Jesus and his return from heaven in the *parousia*. We have seen that these periods are: (1) the ministry of Jesus (3.13-18); (2) the apostolic age (3.19-20); (3) the post-apostolic period (3.21-31); and (4) the time of Roman domination (4.1-13); the expected world transformation following the *parousia* is then described as the climax and antithesis in 4.14-18. The First Vision is introduced by the statement that Beliar was angry with Isaiah because of the prophet's exposure of Sammael (3.13). This is a way of saying that the Ascension of Isaiah predicted the overthrow of authorities hostile to the author and his friends.

3.13-18 narrates the life of Jesus and sets his story within the framework of the Beloved One's descent from heaven. The author mentions the Beloved's 'coming' from the seventh heaven and he uses the noun 'transformation' to describe this earthly appearance (3.13). This is repeated in the statement that the Beloved was transformed 'into human likeness'. The explicit notion of 'transformation' represents a significant difference from first-century christology. Where the mediator's descent from heaven had been a feature of Johannine christology (see Jn 3.13), and perhaps even of Pauline (in Phil. 2.5-11), the Ascension of Isaiah develops this view by including a more extensive mythological scheme which involves the mediator's commission by God in the seventh heaven (10.6-17), his disguised descent (10.17-31) and transformation into the person of Jesus, followed by his return to heaven in the ascension (3.18; 11.23-33). There are parallels for this mythological scheme in the Jewish angelophanic tradition, especially perhaps in the description of the angel Raphael in the book of Tobit. The author evidently knew such material and used it to develop his portrait of Jesus in the way that is described here.

This mythological scheme yields the suggestion that Jesus was the temporary appearance of the Beloved One who had assumed human form. The author mentions his tormenting by the 'children of Israel' (3.13; for the phrase cf. Mt. 27.25); the coming of the twelve disciples; the teaching; his crucifixion; his crucifixion with wicked men; his burial in the grave (all 3.13); the offence of the twelve (3.14); the guards at the tomb (3.14; cf. Mt. 27.62-66); and the descent from heaven of the 'angel of the Church' (3.15). The latter is a Semitizing expression which attributes angelomorphic existence to the church as if it were a pre-existent entity. 3.16-17 is a striking (Jewish-Christian) account of the resurrection:

> The angel of the Holy Spirit and Michael, the chief of the holy angels, will open his grave on the third day, and that Beloved, sitting on their shoulders, will come forth.

This passage preserves the tradition of the empty tomb (found in the Gospels but not in Paul). Unlike the Gospels, however, the Ascension of Isaiah attempts to explain what happened in the resurrection and it reveals a more speculative interest in this matter than that displayed by the literature of first-century Christianity. We do not know how old or reliable this account is; the only other witness to it is the Gospel of Peter (39) which may be dependent on the Ascension of Isaiah (c.150 CE). At the heart of the story may lie the tradition, recorded by Luke (24.4) and John (20.12-13), that two angels attended the empty tomb. The apocalypse represents either an exegetical development of that story or a separate tradition altogether.

3. A Commentary on the Ascension of Isaiah 55

The fact that Michael and the Spirit escort the Beloved shoulder-high in triumph from the tomb demonstrates the mediator's unequalled position in respect of other heavenly beings. This is the real point of the story. The Beloved One in the Ascension of Isaiah is subordinate only to God whose worship he shares (7.17). This portrait of a seated figure attended by angels (3.16-17) anticipates the angelic hierarchy Isaiah would see in the middle heavens, where a seated angel was surrounded by angels on either side (ch. 7), and the prophet's vision of the three divine beings in 11.32-33. The conception has its origin in Jewish throne-mysticism (see Daniélou 1964: 254-55) and it depicts the Beloved One in the same majestic pose as Old Testament theophanic passages depict God (1 Kgs 22.19; Isa. 6.1-7; Ezek. 1.26-27; cf. 1 En. 14; 'theophany' means 'a manifestation or appearance of God'). Asc. Isa. 3.16-17 is thus apparently an early way in which Jewish Christians conceived of their Saviour, as a subordinate divine being who ranked above the angels.

There is a lacuna in the Greek text of 3.16 before the words 'the angel of the Holy Spirit'. At the beginning of the century Grenfell and Hunt restored this lacuna with the angelic name Gabriel to provide a form of parallelism with the reference to Michael (see Charles 1900: 19-20). This reconstruction is not confirmed by the Ethiopic text and so remains speculative, but it is true that in the Ascension of Isaiah the angel of the Holy Spirit discharges some of the functions associated with Gabriel in Judaism, notably in 7.23 that of conveying the souls of the righteous to God. If the restoration is a correct one it would imply that Michael and Gabriel traditions in Judaism served among the sources for the emerging Christian doctrine of the Trinity. The Spirit's frequent designation as an 'angel' tends to confirm that angelology was an important source in this respect.

3.17b-18 then states that the Beloved One would send out his twelve disciples (3.17; Gk omits this figure) who would teach 'all nations and every tongue' the resurrection of the Beloved (3.18). 'Those who believed in his cross' would be saved (3.18; cf. 9.24-26). This phrase anticipates the soteriology expressed in ch. 10 where the Beloved's victory over Beliar is associated especially with his death. It reminds readers of the need to believe that the Beloved One had defeated Beliar and it provides a link with the later material. The Beloved's ministry would conclude with his ascension ('resurrection' in the Ethiopic text; cf. 10.14) to the seventh heaven 'from where he came' (3.18; cf. Jn 6.62),

The question has been raised of what sources lie behind the description of the life of Jesus found in 3.13-18 and 11.2-22 (Ethiopic text). Both passages shows signs of affinity to Matthew's special material but the description of the resurrection in 3.16-17 and the statement about the absent midwife in 11.14a draw on traditions that are not found in any of the Gospels. It has been suggested that this material was taken from summaries of the life of Jesus, similar to those used also by the author of Acts, which derived from the oral tradition that circulated before the Gospels were written. This suggestion has been made in unpublished papers independently by R.J. Bauckham and E. Norelli. The author of the Ascension of Isaiah probably knew Matthew's Gospel but it seems likely that he took the material about Jesus from such an oral source. The Ascension of Isaiah thus probably shows the wider material that was lost when the oral tradition about Jesus died out and left only written texts.

The life of Jesus is followed in the author's scheme by a short description of the apostolic age (3.19-20). This is presented as a time when many Christians spoke 'through the Holy Spirit' and when 'signs and miracles' abounded. The author emphasizes the charismatic aspect of the apostolic age to draw attention to the way in which he believed that the Holy Spirit was being suppressed in his own day (see 3.26b-28).

The Church Leaders Oppose the Prophets

The author's sense of distance from the apostolic age is revealed by 3.21. This verse says that 'afterwards', 'at his [the Beloved's] approach', his disciples would 'abandon the teaching of the twelve apostles, and their faith, and their love, and their purity'. No specific heresy (christological or otherwise) is mentioned by the Ascension of Isaiah and the author would have agreed with Ignatius in insisting that the Beloved was really born and that he genuinely died on the cross. The primary focus of this criticism is ethical (see Charlesworth 1981: 41-46) but the way in which the author criticizes people for making friends with the world (3.25) and emphasizes the parousia hope (4.14) suggests that eschatological scepticism may also have been an issue which he felt the need to confront. 2 Pet. 3.4-7 (late first or early second century CE) similarly addresses a situation in which people had begun to question the hope for Christ's return (see also 1 Clem. 23.3-4 and 2 Clem. 11.2-4). The Ascension of Isaiah attacks those who 'made ineffective' the

3. A Commentary on the Ascension of Isaiah   57

prophetic oracles (3.31), which as we can see from the First Vision contained warnings about eschatological judgment (see 4.18; cf. 2 Pet. 2.1-22). Eschatological questions would have been posed acutely in the second century in view of the belief inherited from first-century Christianity that the parousia was near, and what seemed to be the worrying delay of this event. The author's interest in the Ascension of Isaiah lies in part in providing assurance about the future parousia, which is presented as the event by which the Romans' arrogance would be thwarted. The pseudonymous setting of the apocalypse helped to lend credibility to this view, as no doubt did the circle's continuing experience of mysticism.

3.21-31 has no exact parallels in other Christian literature and evidently represents the author's view of the church in his own day. He speaks of 'contention' (Gk has 'heresies' in the sense of 'parties') and states that many loved office but that they lacked the wisdom needed to discharge it (3.23). This directs the focus of the criticism in 3.21-31 to office-holders in the church. That it is the church leaders who are criticized in this section is confirmed by the reference to 'wicked elders and shepherds' in 3.24. The fact that traditional apocalyptic language undergirds this section (cf. Ezek. 34; 1 En. 89.61-65) perhaps explains why the author does not use the technical 'bishop-presbyter-deacon' terminology found in Ignatius or the 'bishop-deacon' configuration of Did. 15.1 The situation revealed here is one in which 'shepherds and elders' were well-known figures in Christian churches and in which they vied among each other for authority in them. This worked to the disadvantage of the prophets, who were scorned in this search for authority (3.31).

In 3.25 the author complains that many had exchanged 'the glory of the robes of the saints' (perhaps a recognition that many Christians came from the poorer classes; cf. Jeffers 1991: 3-35) for the clothes of 'those who loved money'. While this verse is difficult to interpret it suggests that some Christians were trying to improve their social position. This was done by 'respect of persons'; that phrase probably denotes the attempt to curry favour with those in authority, and perhaps also the willingness to compromise with Rome's demands in the manner suggested by ch. 4. Such people are called 'lovers of the glory of this world'. The imminent eschatology of 4.14 is in part set against this attitude and it makes social improvement irrelevant in view of the impending change. 3.25 is an important source for early Christian social history. It reveals a situation in which adherents of the new religion were trying to adjust to a world order that was proving more durable than the earliest Christian preaching had envisaged. The author states that many Christians were successfully adjusting in this way, but his apocalypse also shows that second-century Christianity was capable of asserting a fervent millenarian hope (with the qualification noted here about the Second Vision).

3.26 mentions 'many slanderers and [much] vainglory at the approach of the Lord'; the author states that 'the Holy Spirit will withdraw from many' (3.26b). 'Slander' means speaking evil of other people (rather than blasphemy against the Holy Spirit). It is a familiar complaint in early Christian literature (see e.g. 1 Clem. 30.1; 2 Clem. 4.3; Herm. Man. 2.3). The notion that the Spirit had withdrawn from many (a very strong statement) shows the grounds of the author's complaint against the church leaders, as argued already in this Guide: their prominence meant that the prophets' authority had been curbed. This complaint is amplified in 3.27 by the statement about the paucity of prophets and of those who spoke reliable words. The author adds the comment 'except one here and there in different places' which evidently designates himself and his friends (cf 2.7, 9; 6.14, 17). 3.28 then says that prophetic influence had waned 'because of the spirit of error and of fornication, and of vainglory, and of the love of money...among those who are said to be servants of that One'. What is said here recalls some of the vices attributed to Manasseh at the beginning of ch. 2, as if the author saw analogies between the narrative situation that he describes in the apocalypse and events in the church of his own day.

3.29 mentions the 'great hatred' which existed among the 'shepherds and elders' at the time. There is evidence in the letters of Ignatius that disputes about authority were known in Christianity at the time (see Schoedel 1985: 13-14 for an evaluation of this evidence). The author of the Ascension of Isaiah links such behaviour to the 'great jealousy in the last days' and he claims that a person now spoke 'whatever pleased him in his own eyes' (3.30), as opposed no doubt to genuine inspiration by the Spirit. 3.31 says that people would 'make ineffective' the prophecy of the prophets before Isaiah and Isaiah's visions as well. While the phrase 'make ineffective' is not further defined, in the light of 3.21-31 it seems to reflect an attempt by more powerful Christians, in this context doubtless the 'shepherds and elders' of 3.29, to silence the prophets as Manasseh would do in ch. 5. This was because they represented rival claimants to authority. Asc. Isa. 3.31 evidently describes an act of repression experienced by someone known to the readers, perhaps by the author of the apocalypse himself.

Rome Makes Demands for Obedience

The author turns to problems beyond the church in ch. 4. This passage supplies the reason why the Ascension of Isaiah was written. There he states that Beliar, 'the king of this world, which he has ruled over ever since it existed' (cf. 7.9-12), would 'descend from the firmament in the form of a man, a king of iniquity, a murderer of his mother' (4.2). This is an allusion to the myth of Nero's return, sometimes called the myth of Nero *redivivus*, which is found in diverse forms in classical and Jewish literature that describes the period between the emperor's death in 68 CE and the end of the Second Jewish Revolt against Rome in 135 CE. Evidence for this myth is found in Tacitus, *Hist.* 2.8 and Dio Cassius 64.9, and in Judaeo-Christian literature, especially in the Sibylline Oracles. The return of Beliar in the form of Nero is mentioned in Sib. Or. 3.63-74:

> Then Beliar will come from the *Sebastenoi*,
> and he will raise up the height of mountains, he will raise up the sea,
> the great fiery sun and shining moon,
> for men. But they will not be effective in him.
> But he will, indeed, also lead men astray, and he will lead astray
> many faithful, chosen Hebrews, and also other lawless men
> who have not yet listened to the word of God.
> But whenever the threats of the great God draws nigh
> and a burning power comes through the sea to land
> it will also burn Beliar and all overbearing men,
> as many as put their faith in him (translation in Collins 1983).

This part of the book was added at some stage after 70 CE but it is difficult to say precisely when. It was probably dependent on the same source that was used by the author of the Ascension of Isaiah. The return of Nero is also mentioned in Sibylline Oracle 5, which reached its final form in the reign of Hadrian:

> But the one who obtained the land of the Persians will fight,
> and killing every man he will destroy all life
> so that a one-third portion will remain for wretched mortals.
> He himself will rush in with a light bound from the West,
> besieging the entire land, laying it all waste' (Sib. Or. 5.101-04;
> for the interpretation of this material see Collins 1974: 80-87).

The form of mythology used in the Ascension of Isaiah assumes that Nero's return would be a posthumous one. This sets the apocalypse after the emperor's death, and the Ascension of Isaiah may have been written perhaps as much as sixty years after that event. The author of the Ascension of Isaiah fuses together mythology about Nero with material that describes Beliar's descent from the firmament, which he evidently developed from the Christian belief, found in Lk 10.18 and Rev. 12.9, that Satan had been cast down from heaven to earth. This fusion of mythology in ch. 4 shows the author's hostility to the experience of Roman domination and it was intended to criticize the Romans' imposition of the sacrifice test by presenting the imperial government in demonic terms. This allusion to demonic opposition would have been understood by a Christian readership who were accustomed to the belief that an eschatological opponent would appear before Jesus returned (see 2 Thess. 2.1-10; cf. Rev. 13 and 17).

4.3 mentions the Neronian Persecution (64 CE) as a foil for Rome's future behaviour. The Ethiopic text says that Nero would 'persecute the plant which the twelve apostles of the Beloved will have planted; some of the twelve will be given into his hand'. This looks back to the first century, although the prophecy is in the future tense as befits the pseudonymous setting. The Greek version is more precise than the Ethiopic and states that 'one' of the twelve would be given into his hand; this is generally taken as an allusion to Peter's martyrdom at Rome in 64 CE (cf. also 1 Clem. 5.4; Ign. Rom. 4.3). 4.4 then anticipates Nero's reappearance: 'This angel, Beliar, will come in the form of that king, and with him will come all the powers of this world, and they will obey him in every wish'. The emphasis falls in this on Beliar's presence in the Roman authorities rather than on the literal belief that Nero would reappear from beyond the grave. The statement is a way of describing the new phase of relations with the Roman government that began in the second century CE but it draws on earlier imagery.

4.5 continues this theme and mentions Beliar's mastery over the sun and moon which would rise at unnatural times (cf. Sib. Or. 3.63-65 cited above). According to 4.6 Beliar would have absolute sway in the world and would act and speak like the Beloved One. He would claim, in words parodied from Isa. 45.18, that 'I am the Lord, and before me there was no one'. The same words are spoken by the angels in the firmament in 10.13 and they show the blasphemy of the Roman government in making demands for homage. Their original speaker had been the Jewish God in Isaiah 45. The fact that they are here applied to a lesser being (the demon in the firmament) who denied God's existence shows the sense of irony which undergirds Asc. Isa. 4.6 and which forms part of the author's response to the crisis. This irony is intensified by the cosmology which emphasizes Beliar's distance from the supreme God and his exclusion from the heavenly world. These lines from Isaiah 45 would later be spoken by the Gnostic Demiurge in the Apocryphon of John. The Ascension of Isaiah may have offered ideas to Gnostic writers, but it is important to make the point that the apocalypse is not a Gnostic text as such.

It is difficult to miss a reference in ch. 4 to a situation of conflict between Christians and Romans like that found in second century Bithynia (but we do not know how much later than 112 CE the apocalypse was written). This is especially evident in 4.7-11, a passage which expresses further criticism of Rome. 4.7 ('all men in the world will believe in him') shows what was seen as the invincible nature of Roman power at the time. 4.8 ('they will sacrifice to him and serve him') probably refers to the sacrifice test, especially Pliny's demand to offer incense before the statues produced in court. 4.9 expects that many Christians would follow Beliar (the prophets are the evident exceptions). 4.10 anticipates spurious miracles performed by Beliar, something that earlier Christian literature had associated with the activity of the eschatological opponent (see 2 Thess. 2.9-10). 4.11 ('He will set up his image before him in every city') again reflects the Bithynian situation and seems to be a further reference to the demand for reverence addressed to the imperial statue.

4.12 sets a precise limit on Beliar's reign. The author states that he would rule for 'three years, seven months and twenty-seven days', that is the 1335 days of Dan. 12.12 reckoned according to the Julian calendar. The author of the Ascension of Isaiah evidently knew the book of Daniel and used it extensively because Daniel had described a similar situation of conflict with an occupying power that involved what were regarded as inappropriate religious demands. 4.13 is a difficult verse to interpret. Some have taken it as an indication that a few of the original eyewitnesses of Jesus were still alive. This conclusion must be qualified through observing that the focus of the verse is not so much on the survival of the original generation as on the assertion that few would be left *as the Beloved's servants* in view of the apostasy anticipated by 4.9. These faithful ones would 'flee from desert to desert' as they awaited the millenarian kingdom (4.13). The statement that they were 'few' recalls the description of Isaiah's wilderness community in

2.7-11 and the reference to 'one here and there in different places' (3.27). It also recalls the Old Testament idea of the faithful remnant in Israel (see e.g. Isa. 37.32) and it shows the author's view that the prophets alone remained faithful at the time. While the desert might be seen as a place of safety (1 Kgs 17.2; 1 Macc. 2.28-30; Rev. 12.6, 14) it was also the place where messianic movements were formed (see Mt. 3.1-12; Acts 21.38). According to Asc. Isa. 2.9 it was moreover the place where apocalyptic revelation occurred, so that the phrase as used here is a suggestive one

The thought of 4.13 is thus that the faithful few should retreat to the desert until the Beloved One returned to introduce his kingdom. This seems to be a way of advocating caution towards too ready an engagement with the Romans (cf. 5.13) and it also affirms the importance of continuing apocalyptic activity and eschatological hope. The date for the Ascension of Isaiah suggested in this Guide makes it unlikely that any of the original disciples would have been alive at the time of writing.

The Expression of Hope in the First Vision

4.14-18 represents the climax of the First Vision. Here the author expresses his hope that the Beloved One would return from heaven to introduce a completely different situation. This new situation was to be the temporary earthly kingdom which would precede a permanent life in the seventh heaven. 4.14, which exists only in the Ethiopic version, states that the Beloved would return after 'three hundred and thirty two days'; the figure of a thousand has clearly dropped out here and is rightly restored by commentators. It has been argued that the 'thirty-two' is a mistake for 'thirty-five'; the figure then agrees with 4.12 as we should expect. This hope for the *parousia* is expressed in language that was derived ultimately from Zech. 14.5 ('the Lord my God will come with all the holy ones'), but Paul in 1 Thess. 3.13 and 2 Thess. 1.7 (especially the latter) was probably a mediating source for this passage. Asc. Isa. 4.14 attributes to the Beloved One activity which the Old Testament text had assigned to God. Such use of the Old Testament, particularly of its theophanic passages, was one of the ways in which early Christianity confirmed its beliefs about the divinity and *parousia* of Jesus.

The returning Beloved One was expected to drag Beliar into Gehenna. Gehenna was the place of eternal punishment in Jewish apocalyptic literature (cf. 1 En. 90.26; 4 Ezra 7.36; 2 Bar. 59.10; Sib. Or. 4.186). Later in the Ascension of Isaiah (10.8) the author distinguishes between Sheol (the place of the dead) and Haguel (the place of final perdition); Gehenna here is the equivalent of Haguel there. The thought of this passage is that the Beloved would remove Beliar permanently from the earth so that his influence would no longer be felt in the human world. Since the author believed that Beliar stood behind the Roman Empire (4.4) the demon's demise would mean the end of the situation which the author found difficult including the problem of investigation by the Romans. The result of this intervention would be that those who had been oppressed would be given 'rest' (4.15). Asc. Isa. 4.14-18 stands in a tradition of Christian eschatology, with its roots in Jewish apocalyptic, which anticipated the establishment of the messiah's earthly kingdom over which he would personally reign (cf. 1 Cor. 15.24-28). The author of the Ascension of Isaiah says that only the 'saints' would share in this kingdom. Beliar's 'hosts' would perish with their master (4.14). Into this last category fall the Romans and possibly the apostate Christians as well.

The hope for 'rest' (4.15) looks back to 2 Thess. 1.6-7 which evidently served as the source for this passage. It is an important aspect of the work's eschatology that even those who had died would descend from heaven to share in the kingdom (4.16). This belief assumes that the departed enjoyed a temporary existence in heaven from which they would descend to live once more in a human body. The Ascension of Isaiah sets itself firmly against the notion of corporeality when describing the final resurrection state, however. The ultimate destiny of the righteous was to ascend to the seventh heaven as their bodies were left behind in the world (4.17). In this way the author distinguishes between different kinds of resurrection, as did the author of Revelation (20.5), and he asserts that the final destiny of the faithful was to be with God in the seventh heaven (cf. 9.37-38).

The end of the world would involve a full-scale destruction in which the Beloved's voice would angrily reprove heaven, earth, mountains, hills, cities, desert, trees and even the elements ('the angel of the sun...and moon'), and everywhere that had permitted Beliar's domination. There would be a resurrection and a judgment (4.18). This statement seems a little awkward in view of the reference to immortality in 4.17 but it is based perhaps on the double-edged resurrection hope suggested by Dan. 12.2, where some were expected to rise to everlasting life but others to shame and contempt. The Beloved would cause fire to rise from him which would consume all the impious, who would be as if they had never been created (4.18). The end of the world as the author saw it would thus involve a return to primeval conditions in which the righteous would be safely gathered into heaven and the ungodly punished without mercy. There is nothing here to match the notion of a new heaven and earth (or of the renewed Jerusalem) found in Revelation 21.

4.19 states that the 'rest of the words of the vision' were written in the vision of Babylon. This is an allusion to Isaiah 13, a prophecy of vengeance against the enemies of Israel. The rest of ch. 4 explains that the Beloved's activity was predicted in writings from the second and third divisions of the Jewish Bible—but any reference to the Torah is strikingly absent (cf. 3.8-10). 4.20 says that the whole of Isaiah contained visions of the Beloved One. This verse implies a distinction between the canonical prophecy as the 'book which I prophesied openly' and the Ascension of Isaiah as an apocalypse which contained esoteric information about the Beloved One. 4.21 understands Isa. 52.13–53.12 to predict the Beloved One's descent to Sheol. 4.21-22 adds the Prophets and the Writings (the second and third divisions of the Hebrew Bible) to the list of witnesses about the Beloved One. The passage ends with a reference to 'the words of the righteous Joseph,' which some think designates the Jewish mystical writing called the Prayer of Joseph (in which the patriarch Jacob is identified with the angel Israel; see Smith 1985). Although this identification remains uncertain it is an attractive one because the Prayer of Joseph, like the Ascension of Isaiah, draws on angelology to identify a human person with an exalted heavenly being. This reference would then tend to confirm that Jewish angelology was an important source for the Ascension of Isaiah's christology.

The Prophet's Martyrdom

Chapter 5 resumes the narrative of Isaiah's martyrdom. The context of this material, which comes after Isaiah's arrest (3.12) and the First Vision, indicates that it was for his witness to the Beloved One that the prophet was killed. The author says that Beliar was angry with Isaiah because of his visions and because the demon dwelt in Manasseh's heart (cf. 2.1); Manasseh then sawed Isaiah in half with a wood-saw (5.1). Knibb thinks that the phrase 'wood-saw' represents a Hebrew construct formula and that the work called the Martyrdom of Isaiah was originally written in Hebrew (1985: 146). If, however, the author relied merely on oral tradition the most that we can say is that the legend probably circulated in Hebrew.

As Isaiah was dying, Belchira and all the false prophets stood by and mocked his misfortune (5.2). In 5.3-6 Belchira offered Isaiah an opportunity to save his life if he would admit to being a liar and say that the ways of Manasseh and his associates were upright. This is tantamount to the demand for a Christian prophet to say that Rome was justified in its demands. Isaiah was absorbed in a vision of the Lord (5.7), like Stephen in Acts 7.55. Belchira repeated his offer of safety and stated that he would make Manasseh and the princes of Judah worship Isaiah if he withdrew what he had said (5.8; the verse makes allusion to the temptation of Jesus). Isaiah scornfully refused this offer. He cursed Belchira and his hosts (5.9) and stated that they could take only the skin of his body (5.10). This description of the Christian prophet on trial for his faith parallels the Bithynian situation, and Isaiah's cursing of the demon resembles a Christian response to the demand to curse Christ required by Pliny's sacrifice test.

The execution continued as the prophet's opponents looked on (5.11-12). Isaiah dismissed the prophets who were with him and sent them to Tyre and Sidon with the explanation that for him alone God had mixed the cup (5.13). This comment is based on the words of Jesus in Mt. 20.22 and 26.39. Isaiah's dismissal of the other prophets seems to be the author's way of suggesting that Christians should not court disaster by coming to Roman attention unnecessarily, and it is probably to be read in conjunction with the material in 2.7-11 and 4.13 as a warning against voluntary martyrdom. Isaiah did not cry out as he was being sawn in two but spoke with the Spirit until he died (5.14). The author states that Beliar did this to Isaiah because Sammael was angry about his visions of the Beloved One, particularly his predictions of Sammael's destruction (5.15-16).

The view taken here is that 5.13 advocates caution against unnecessary involvement with the Romans. Voluntary martyrdom, the reckless acceptance of death for religious belief, was a significant feature of some Christian circles in the second and third centuries. Ignatius had been preoccupied with his impending death and he begged the Roman Christians to do nothing to prevent it (Ign. Rom. 4.1). The statement of 4.13 that the faithful must occupy the desert, which recalls the description of the isolated prophetic community in 2.7-11, hints that prudent withdrawal was preferable in the author's view to deliberate self-sacrifice. The author may have feared that some readers would seek death with lurid anticipation, like Ignatius who compared himself to the wheat of God that would be ground by the wild beasts (Ign. Rom. 4.1). The Ascension of Isaiah praises the piety of someone who found no escape but warns that Isaiah's death was sacrifice enough. It is possible that the death of Ignatius inspired ch. 5 to some degree. The apocalypse thus adopts a cautionary stance towards the problem of relations with the Romans. Its readers were left in no doubt about what Rome might do, and they were warned of the need for withdrawal should such investigation occur.

The Second Vision

There is a marked change of tone at the beginning of ch. 6, where what is here called the 'Second Vision' begins. The Second Vision is an account of Isaiah's mystical ascension to the seventh heaven in which he saw the Beloved One's descent and his victory over Beliar. The Second Vision lacks the earlier emphasis on the imminent millenarian kingdom. Instead, the author offers an interpretation of the death of Jesus in which what the Beloved had done in the past is made the grounds for hope in salvation.

The narrative describes how Isaiah came to Jerusalem from Gilgal with Josab (6.1). He reclined on the king's couch in anticipation of mystical revelation (6.2). The prophet began to speak the 'words of faith and righteousness' with Hezekiah as the royal court assembled (6.3). Forty prophets and sons of the prophets had come from the neighbouring districts when they learned of Isaiah's arrival. These had come to greet him and hear his words (6.4) and in order that he might lay his hands on them, so that they could prophesy and he could test what they said (6.5). The author alludes here to a rite of prophetic ordination in which the process of discernment was a significant feature. If the chapter in any way reflects the practices of the author's circle such ordination may have been part of the attempt to preserve prophetic activity at a time when it was falling into decline (cf. 3.21-31). The impression gained from the passage is that prophecy was now made subject to careful control in order to ensure its safe transmission to younger practitioners.

Hall (1990) sees ch. 6 as suggesting a regular meeting of prophets from different communities, and this is perhaps not unlikely. It was in the context of such a gathering that Isaiah's ascension occurred. The

3. A Commentary on the Ascension of Isaiah 67

narrative gives the impression that it was written with actual experience of mysticism in the author's mind. As Isaiah was speaking 'the words of faith and righteousness' with Hezekiah (6.6) all those present heard a door being opened (in heaven; cf. Rev. 4.1) and the voice of the Holy Spirit (speaking through Isa; cf. 6.10). The narrative is somewhat repetitive, probably because it has been overworked in the course of transmission (cf. Ezek. 1 and 1 En. 14, where reworking also seems likely). The king summoned everybody; the prophets sat on his right (6.7; for the names cf. 2.9). All heard the voice of the Spirit and worshipped God (6.8) who had 'given a door in an alien world' to a human being (6.9).

While Isaiah was speaking in the Spirit he fell silent and his mind was taken up from him; he no longer saw those surrounding him (6.10; cf. Acts 9.8). His eyes were open but his mouth was silent as the 'mind in his body was taken up from him' (6.11). His breath was still in him but he witnessed a vision (6.12). His ascension was said to be assisted by an angel companion (6.13) who came from the seventh heaven (a figure often called the *angelus interpres* in scholarly literature). This introduction to the Second Vision suggests that Isaiah entered some form of cataleptic trance in which his body remained inert on the ground while in his imagination the mystic thought that he ascended through the heavens to the presence of God.

The later verses of ch. 6 create the impression that the revelation was intended only for a select group of people. 6.14 says that the majority did not think that Isaiah had been taken up in this way. 6.17 adds that only the 'doers of righteousness' and those who had the 'fragrance of the Spirit' (i.e. the prophets) saw the vision; the 'officials...eunuchs... and the people' were dismissed from the courtroom when Isaiah entered his trance. This sense of exclusivity reflects the author's belief that only the prophets remained faithful at the time (cf. 2.7-11; 3.21-31). He seems to have suspected the integrity of Christians who did not persist with apocalyptic activity on the grounds that these had suppressed the voice of the Spirit (cf. 3.26-27). This explains why the Second Vision should be reserved for the prophets alone.

There is an interesting analogy to what is said here about Isaiah's mystical experience in the later Jewish writing called *Hekhaloth Rabbati*. This text describes how a mystic told his disciples what was happening to him as he made a heavenly ascension (see Gruenwald 1980: 150-73). The description of Isaiah lying on the royal couch surrounded by the other prophets suggests that a similar understanding may undergird this report. We are perhaps to think of a gathering of Christian prophets who practised mystical ascension to gain reassurance about their faith at what was proving to be a difficult time. The mystical confirmation that the Beloved One had defeated Beliar provided them with security in the face of harrassment from the Roman government.

Isaiah's Ascension through the Seven Heavens

The description of Isaiah's mystical ascension begins in 7.1. What Isaiah sees in the lower heavens prepares him for his vision of the Beloved's descent in chs. 10–11. 7.2 shifts from the third person to the first person narrator which suggests that the material incorporates authentic mystical experience. Isaiah saw a glorious angel (7.2; cf. 2 En. 1.4) who took him by the hand (7.3) and promised a heavenly journey (7.3-6). 7.7-8 is an important passage for interpreting the work's christology, and here study of the different versions is important. The Ethiopic, which is supported by L1 and S (cf. GL 2.7), presents a binitarian reference that promises Isaiah a vision of 'one greater than me'—'me' denotes Isaiah's companion angel—and of 'the Father of the one who is greater'. L2 seems more monotheistic and apparently omits a reference to the second figure but the text is corrupt and this makes the issue difficult to decide. 7.7-8 on the balance of evidence promises Isaiah a binitarian vision in the seventh heaven, one in which God was attended by the Beloved One as a second divine figure.

This mystical christology has a background in Jewish visions of God which gave prominence to an angel who functioned as God's chief agent. Christians modified this view by making the heavenly Christ a second divine being and by offering him worship (see Hurtado 1988: 93-124), but the fact that the Beloved is here described as 'one greater than me' suggests that an angelomorphic christology is an important feature of the Ascension of Isaiah ('angelomorphic christology' denotes the author's portrayal of the Beloved One in imagery which is derived from angelology but which recognizes that he is a divine being).

Isaiah journeyed through the firmament or sky in 7.9-12. This was the region, juxtaposed between heaven and earth, where Sammael ('Satan', S, L2, GL 2.9) or Beliar dwelt. The prophet saw a great struggle there, together with 'the words of Satan', and observed how the angels there envied one another (7.9). He related this to human conflict: 'And as above, so also on earth, for the likeness of what [is] in the firmament is here on earth' (7.10). This comment picks up the dualism of the earlier chapters which referred human behaviour to belief in a particular divinity, but the author does not offer a precise explanation of how events in the firmament corresponded to those on earth. The passage is probably intended to recall the association between Beliar and the Roman emperor made by ch. 4 and thus to make the point that Beliar was the 'king of this world', as he is called there (cf. also 10.12-13). Isaiah asked about the reason for this angelic envying (7.11) and was told that it had been 'ever since the world existed'; his companion said that the struggle would last until 'the one comes whom you are to see, and he will destroy him' (7.12).

7.9-12 effectively says that human struggling and envying, however it manifested itself, was inspired by Beliar. 7.12 is an important passage in the Ascension of Isaiah since it identifies the problem which the Beloved One's descent was undertaken to remedy. This was Beliar's interference in the human world, which worked to the disadvantage of pious Christians and yielded contention since strife. The author reminded readers that many around them had been misled by a demon who had usurped the place of God. The Second Vision offers revealed knowledge about this fact and proposes an alternative understanding—that Beliar had been *destroyed* by the Beloved One—which sets their situation in with its true light.

By comparison with other apocalypses the Ascension of Isaiah is restrained in its description of what the different heavens contain. The reason for this restraint lies in the author's over-riding concern with soteriology, which displaced uranography, metereology and other topics that interested apocalyptic writers (for a description of this wider mystical interest see Stone 1976). The author's soteriological interest explains why so much of the Second Vision contains a description of the Beloved One and his activity, for this was the means by which security had been achieved. The cosmology is also distinctive when compared with other apocalyptic literature. The structure of the middle heavens (ch. 7), in which an enthroned angel sat surrounded by others, suggests that the Ascension of Isaiah was written with a Trinitarian perspective in mind. This scene anticipates Isaiah's vision of the three divine beings in ch. 9. The notion of an individual throne in the heavens is found elsewhere only in the later *merkabah*-midrash called *Re'uyoth Yehezkel* ('The Visions of Ezekiel'; see Gruenwald 1980: 134-41), which seems to be dependent on the Ascension of Isaiah. The Ascension of Isaiah represents a stage of Christian thought in which the need to express belief in three divine beings had become an important concern.

7.13 describes Isaiah's entry into the first heaven. The prophet saw a throne which was surrounded on either side by angels (7.14). The angels on the right are said to be more glorious than those on the left and to offer better praises to God (7.15). Isaiah was told that their worship was directed 'to the praise of [the One who sits in] the seventh heaven...and to his Beloved' (7.17), in a further binitarian reference. He saw a similar scene in the second to fifth heaven except that the central throne was occupied by an angel who was said to be more glorious than the other angels.

When Isaiah entered the second heaven he fell before the enthroned angel as if to offer him worship, but was told not to do this by his companion (7.21). The similarity between this passage and Rev. 19.10; 22.8-9 suggests that the author was drawing on an apocalyptic tradition which had recognized the dangers of angel-worship (see Bauckham 1980-1981). Isaiah was promised that his own throne had been placed 'above all the heavens and their angels' (7.22; cf. 4.17). In the third heaven (7.24-27) Isaiah saw a similar scene (7.24), and observed that 'the glory of his face' was being transformed (7.25). He was told that no mention of the world was made there (this emphasizes the transcendence of the revelation) but that nothing done there was hidden from that region (7.25, cf. 9.19-23). Thus the prophet passed through the fourth (7.28-31) and fifth (7.32-37) heavens and saw the seated angel surrounded by the others, all of whom took their part in the heavenly liturgy. Isaiah observed the great distance between the third and fourth heavens (7.28) and praised the One who had ordered things so (7.37).

The impression that the author was describing a transcendent mystery is reinforced by the fact that the sixth heaven had an atmosphere through which he had to pass before entry (8.1). Isaiah saw a splendour there that he had not witnessed previously and marvelled at the glory of the angels (8.2). When he called the companion angel 'my lord' he was reminded that he was simply his companion (8.5), which recalls the prohibition of angel worship made by 7.21. Isaiah was told that there were neither groups of angels nor a throne placed in the middle of that heaven because the angels were directed by 'the power of the seventh heaven, where the One who is not named dwells, and his Chosen One, whose name is unknown' (8.7). The Beloved's descent was then predicted: Isaiah was told that he would see 'the Lord of all these heavens and of these thrones' (the title applies to the Beloved One) being transformed until he resembled human likeness (8.9-10; cf. 3.13). The prophet was reminded that he was seeing something that nobody had seen before (8.11), perhaps a response to other Christians who were criticizing the practice of mystical ascension (Jn 3.13 makes for an interesting comparison here). Isaiah was promised that he would receive a heavenly garment when he entered the seventh heaven (8.14-15; cf. 9.24-26).

Isaiah entered the sixth heaven itself (8.16-28) and sang praises with the angels there (8.17). He asked the angel if he could stay there permanently but was told that the time of his death had not yet arrived (8.25-28) and that he must return to the earth. The conclusion of the apocalypse, however, promises that he would return to the seventh heaven (11.35)

Isaiah's Vision of the Seventh Heaven

9.1 describes how Isaiah entered the air of the seventh heaven and how he was accosted by the angel chorus-master of the sixth heaven who tried to prevent his further ascension. This reflects the theme found in Jewish mystical literature of angelic hostility to the seer's ascension, perhaps because transformed human beings could gaze on God which angels might not do (see 9.37-38). The prophet was admitted to the seventh heaven when the Beloved One offered him a heavenly garment (9.2). The Beloved was then identified by a catena of titles as 'your Lord, the Lord, the Lord Christ, who is to be called in the world Jesus' (cf. 10.7). The Slavonic and Latin (L2) translations have an abbreviated version of these titles, a fact which shows their redactional character.

In the seventh heaven Isaiah saw a great light, innumerable angels and the righteous of the antediluvian generation from Adam onwards (9.6-7). The status of these people helps to define the eschatological view presented by the Second Vision. They had already put on their heavenly robes (9.8-9) but they stood beside their thrones and had not yet donned their crowns. Isaiah was told that this was because the Beloved had yet to make his saving journey (9.12). 9.13-17 then offers a further prediction of the descent which sets this statement in perspective. This passage says that the Beloved would descend into the world 'in the last days'. People would 'think that he is flesh and a man' (9.13); they would lay their hand on him and crucify him since they did not know who he was (9.14; cf. 1 Cor. 2.8). In this way his descent would be concealed from the heavens. When he had 'plundered the angel of death' (9.16) he would rise on the third day and remain in the world for 545 days (cf. Irenaeus, *Adv. Haer.* 1.3.2). Isaiah was told that many of the righteous would then ascend with him; all the righteous would receive their robes and crowns when the Beloved had ascended into the seventh heaven (9.17-18).

The effect of this passage is to make the acquisition of heavenly blessings a direct consequence of the Beloved One's saving journey. From the author's perspective this was an accomplished event. Enoch and the others must be presumed to have acquired their crowns and thrones when the Beloved sat next to God (11.32). This material makes the point that everything needed for the security of the faithful had *already* been achieved so that they could have confidence despite what was happening in their lives.

9.19-23 describes how Isaiah saw the heavenly ledgers on which were written the 'deeds of the children of Israel'. Such books are a prominent feature of apocalyptic literature (see Russell 1964: 107-109) and here they are a way of assuring that retribution would take place against those who harried the author and his friends. 9.24-26 further alludes to the robes and crowns stored up for those who 'believed in the cross' (cf. 3.18).

9.27-42 describes Isaiah's vision of the three divine beings. The Beloved is described here as one 'whose glory surpassed that of all' in a context where the 'all' denotes the angels and righteous, so that again the christology has a comparative dimension. All the angels and righteous approached the Beloved One and offered worship; Isaiah joined with them (9.28). The Beloved was then identified as 'the Lord of all the praise which you have seen' (9.32). The title 'Lord' indicates that he was a divine being who received worship with God (cf. 7.17, though the context here is Trinitarian).

There is a textual problem in 9.30. The Latin (L2) and Slavonic translations read the first person singular to state that Isaiah was 'transformed and became like an angel,' where the Ethiopic has the third person to hold that the *Beloved One* was transformed in this way. The Ethiopic constitutes the harder reading and it is to be preferred at this point: it is difficult to see why Isaiah should need further transformation when he had already been given a robe upon entering the seventh heaven in 9.2. Doctrinal considerations explain this alteration in the other versions. The parent of the Latin and Slavonic evidently disliked the suggestion that the Beloved One might resemble the angels and emended the text accordingly. This is confirmed by three references to *Michael* as the most glorious angel, which they have introduced in ch. 9 to deter the suggestion that the Beloved One could be presented in this way (9.23, 29, 42). The Beloved's transformation as recorded by the Ethiopic version was undertaken to aid the prophet's vision and in its context is effectively the first stage in his descent from heaven.

In 9.33-36 the prophet observed the angels worshipping the angel of the Holy Spirit. The Spirit is generally called 'an angel' in the Ascension of Isaiah but 9.33 says that he received angelic worship, so that he must be regarded as a divine being like the Beloved One. The Spirit is here called 'the second angel' and made to stand on the left of the Lord (9.36) in what seems to be a demonstration of his subordination to the Beloved One.

9.37-38 reports how Isaiah saw 'the Great Glory', as God is there called, but the author states that he was unable to gaze on him for more than a moment. Isaiah did, however, see the righteous beholding the divine glory. The angel companion was allowed to see the deity for Isaiah's sake (9.39).

Chapter 9 is distinguished from the closing scene in the Ascension of Isaiah (11.32-33) by the fact that here the Beloved and the Spirit *stand* before the seated deity whereas there they sit on either side of his throne. The fact that the two divinities stand before God at this point is a demonstration of their subordination to him. This is confirmed by 9.40-42 which describes how both led the angels in the worship of God. There is an important ambiguity in the way in which the Beloved One and the angel of the Holy Spirit are portrayed in the Ascension of Isaiah. Although they receive worship from the angels (9.27-36) they must in turn join the angels in worshipping God (9.40-42). This view seems strange to readers accustomed to the later Christian belief that Christ and the Holy Spirit were 'equal in every respect' to God, but the notion that Christ was a subordinate being is frequently found in primitive Christian literature (cf. Jn 14.28). In view of the strong emphasis on the Beloved One's divinity it is significant that this subordinationist aspect should have been retained in the Ascension of Isaiah. The author was apparently concerned to resist any suggestion that there were two or even three Gods (as Paul had done earlier in 1 Cor. 8.6) by refusing to let the Great Glory's supremacy be compromised by the existence of his co-regents.

The Beloved One is Instructed by God to Descend

The heart of the Second Vision is reached in ch. 10. This chapter describes how the Beloved One was commissioned by God and his obedient response in making the descent from the seventh heaven. The author states that Isaiah heard the Most High's voice instructing 'my Lord Christ, who will be called Jesus' (for the titles cf. 9.5 in the Ethiopic text) to descend through the firmament and the world as far as Sheol and to make his likeness like the angels in the five heavens, firmament and Sheol (10.7-16). This passage offers a more detailed explanation of Beliar's activity. It claims to present the words of God, as he told the Beloved that the 'angels of the world' (i.e. Beliar and his angels) were not to know that 'you [are] Lord with me of the seven heavens and of their angels' (10.11), when 'I lift up [my voice] to the sixth heaven, that you may judge and destroy the princes and the angels and the gods of that world, and the world which is ruled by them' (10.12). This punishment is said to be deserved because these angels 'have denied me and said, "We alone are, and there is no one besides us" ' (10.13; cf. 4.6).

No precise definition is offered of how the Beloved One's descent would achieve this judgment of the angels. We can, however, surmise what was the decisive moment by considering the sequence of thought in 10.14-15:

> And *afterwards* you shall ascend from the gods of death to your place, and you shall not be transformed in each of the heavens, but in glory you shall ascend and sit at my right hand, and then the princes and powers of that world will worship you.

The 'afterwards' in this passage denotes the resurrection, as the phrase 'ascending from the gods of death' indicates, and it seems that the resurrection and ascension are understood here as simultaneous events (cf. Phil. 2.9-11). This means that the angels' destruction is in all probability connected with the Beloved's death on the cross, in a way that stands close to the view of the crucifixion expressed by Col. 2.15. The author of the Ascension of Israel and that was probably influenced by that passage at this point. He says that the Beloved's destruction of Beliar would be followed by his ascension to the seventh heaven when the 'princes and the powers of that world' would worship their vanquisher. This was no doubt intended to be taken as a sign of their subjection, and as signifying that salvation had been provided by the events which the Vision describes.

This passage reveals the author's understanding of the achievement of Jesus. It offers an explanation of the incarnation and represents an early view of the atonement which was bound up with the defeat of cosmic powers. The rest of ch. 10 describes how the Beloved responded to this command. From the fifth heaven and downwards he

3. A Commentary on the Ascension of Isaiah 75

was transformed to resemble an angel of those heavens (following his initial transformation in 9.30). The angels there failed to recognize and thus to worship him; he passed unobserved through their midst. He even supplied the password when demanded to conceal his identity (e.g. 10.25). The Beloved descended into the firmament, 'where the prince of this world dwells' (10.29), and supplied the correct password so that the angels did not notice him; 'in envy they were fighting one another, for there is there a power of evil and envying about trifles'. This part of the apocalypse mentions a further group of angels, those in the air (10.30-31), who were 'plundering and doing violence to one another'.

Chapter 11 describes the Beloved One's appearance as Jesus. 11.2-22 in the Ethiopic text includes some traditions about Jesus which are similar to those recorded in 3.13-18. These are omitted by the Slavonic translation and the Latin translation (L2) but the strong probability is that they stood in the original Ascension of Isaiah. The material in 3.13-18 makes for an important comparison with 11.2-22 and confirms that this was so. The Ethiopic text implies that the Beloved descended into the womb of Mary where he was transformed into the infant Jesus—a point that is made more explicitly by the Epistula Apostolorum 13–14 (c. 150 CE—cf. also Sib. Or. 8.456-61).

Mary, like Joseph, is said to be a Davidide (11.2). She was betrothed to Joseph but found to be pregnant before the marriage, and Joseph wanted to leave her (11.3). The angel of the Spirit then appeared in the world (11.4), with the result that Joseph respected Mary's virginity through continence for two months (11.5-6). After that period Mary looked up and saw a small infant, which astonished her (11.8). Her womb was found as before she had conceived; the Ascension of Isaiah offers early evidence for the belief that Mary remained a virgin following the delivery (11.9). Joseph questioned her astonishment but then saw the infant himself (11.10). A heavenly voice forbade them to speak about this (11.11) but the story was soon widely known in Bethlehem (11.12). Some said that Mary had given birth before being married for two months (11.13) while others denied this and said that no midwife had attended her nor had cries of pain been heard (11.14a). 11.14b is the author's own comment, based on a tradition similar to Jn 7.27-28 and perhaps on that passage itself, which states that all were blinded concerning the Beloved One. The author says that they all knew about him but they did not know where he had come from, in a reference to the mediator's heavenly origin.

11.16 then says, in a passage which shares tradition with Ign. Eph. 19.1, that this event (i.e. the incarnation) was hidden from 'all the heavens and all the princes and every god of this world'. According to 11.17 the Beloved 'sucked the breast, as was customary, that he might not be recognized'. This seems to hint that the suckling was undertaken to further the ruse of concealment rather than from genuine need. 11.18 says that the adult Jesus 'performed great signs and miracles in the land of Israel and [in] Jerusalem' and 11.19 describes the crucifixion. The author says that the adversary (i.e. Beliar) envied Jesus and roused the children of Israel against him since they did not know who he was. These handed him to the ruler (i.e. Pilate) and crucified him. The notion that those responsible for the death of Jesus were ignorant of his identity as the Beloved One recalls 1 Cor. 2.8, a passage which the author evidently knew. The author then describes how the Beloved descended to the angel of Sheol at his death. 11.20 further describes the crucifixion, while 11.21 states that he rose again on the third day and remained '(many) days' (cf. 9.16). 11.22 states that he sent out the twelve disciples and ascended.

The Beloved's Ascension and the Conclusion of the Apocalypse

The description of the ascension in 11.22-23 combines the notion of Jesus' physical departure with that of the Beloved One's glorification in the heavens. The first of these views has points in common with the Lukan ascension narrative (Lk. 24.50-52 and Acts 1.9-11) and the second with the christology found in 1 Pet. 3.22. The Beloved One is said to have abandoned his disguise in the ascension so that the angels recognized and worshipped him. Asc. Isa. 11.23-24 describes how he first appeared in the firmament and was instantly recognized by 'all the angels of the firmament, and Satan' who worshipped him. These angels asked how they could have failed to notice the mediator whom they called 'their Lord' in his descent through the heavens (for which the implied answer is that his identity had been concealed). There is a textual problem in 11.24-25, where the Ethiopic translation moves directly to the Beloved's passage through the second heaven and omits any reference to his appearance in the first heaven. We cannot therefore be certain that the words in 11.23-24 were originally spoken by the angels in the firmament but the strong probability remains that they were. The passage demonstrates that angels who had previously denied

3. A Commentary on the Ascension of Isaiah

the existence of God now acknowledged the error of their ways at the appearance of the divine mediator who had come from the seventh heaven. This offering of worship by the demon who inspired the Romans must be set against the background of the sacrifice test, and was part of the author's purpose of creating a situation at variance with reality through which hope was sustained in the Second Vision and the power of the Romans denied.

The Beloved One received angelic worship in all the heavens as he ascended to the seventh heaven. On entering the seventh heaven he took his seat at the right of the throne of God (11.32). The author seems to have derived this notion of the mediator's enthronement at the right hand of God, following his heavenly ascension and the angelic surrender, from a reading of 1 Pet. 3.22, whose author, in company with other Christians (e.g. Paul in Rom. 8.34), had derived the idea from the Septuagintal text of Ps. 110.1. The sequence of thought in Asc. Isa. 11.23-33 and the description of angelic powers in Asc. Isa. 1.3 both suggest that 1 Pet. 3.22 inspired elements of the work's christology. According to 11.33 the Spirit sat on the left of God's throne in what seems to be an extension of the image derived from 1 Pet. 3.22 to yield a Trinitarian view (which may also owe something to an interpretation of Isa. 6.1-4).

In 11.34-35 Isaiah was dismissed from heaven and told to return to his body. The implication of this is that the work of salvation was complete by the time of the Beloved's return to heaven. The Beloved's enthronement is a symbol of Beliar's defeat. This would have had important implications for readers who believed themselves to be faithful disciples of the Beloved One but currently to be oppressed by Beliar.

11.36-43 is a narrative conclusion to the Ascension of Isaiah which reinforces the pseudonymous setting. Isaiah told Hezekiah that 'the end of this world and all this vision will be brought about in the last generation' (11.37-38). This corresponds with the view of Paul (1 Cor. 10.11) and the author of the Qumran Habakkuk Commentary (1QpHab) that Scripture would receive its fulfilment in the eschatological generation, which for both authors meant their own day. Isaiah said that the vision might not be told to the people of Israel and forbade anyone to copy it (11.39). 11.40 links the reception of heavenly benefits (robes, thrones, crowns) with the command to 'be in the Holy Spirit' as if these were seen as a reward for those who kept charismatic influence alive in the church. 11.41 says that Sammael

Satan sawed Isaiah in half because of these visions. 11.42-43 adds that Hezekiah handed this information to Mannaseh in the twenty-sixth year of his reign but that Manasseh did not remember it and became the servant of Satan and was destroyed.

Further Reading

There is no complete English commentary on the Ascension of Isaiah. Caquot has written a commentary on the work's narrative portions (1973), but this takes the view, rejected in this Guide, that the author worked from an earlier Martyrdom of Isaiah. There is a short discussion of the Ascension of Isaiah in Gruenwald 1980: 57-62, and material also in Pesce (ed.) 1983. The fact that this Further Reading section is so short is an indication of the lack of attention that has been accorded the Ascension of Isaiah in scholarly research. The introduction to Knibb's translation (1985) is a welcome exception to this.

4

THE ASCENSION OF ISAIAH AND THEMES IN EARLY CHRISTIANITY

Besides its evidence about life in the second-century church and about the nature of Christian relations with the Romans, the Ascension of Isaiah also sheds light on christology, eschatology, cosmology, Mariology and second-century Gnosticism, but it has received less attention in these areas than it deserves. The exploration of these themes provides the evidence for the view that the Ascension of Isaiah is an important text in the wider study of early Christianity.

Christology

Christology has traditionally been defined as the doctrine of the person and work of Jesus. Both aspects of this definition are reflected in the apocalypse which describes how the Beloved One defeated Beliar through his death on the cross. The Ascension of Isaiah attests a stage of Christian belief in which the desire to present Jesus as divine had led to the incorporation of a mythological scheme which asserted that the heavenly Christ had temporarily transformed himself into human form.

The work's christology has an evident angelomorphic dimension. By this is meant that it presents the Beloved One in language and imagery which the author derived from Jewish angelology but which acknowledges that he was a divine being and not an angel (for a description see Daniélou 1964: 117-46; Longenecker 1970: 26-32). Two strands of evidence support this view about the christology. The notion of the Beloved's heavenly mediation (chs. 9–11) has its background in Jewish apocalyptic visions of angels, some of which describe a mediator in theophanic language. The author of the Ascension of Isaiah also modelled his description of the Beloved One's descent (chs. 10–11) on an angelophany.

The Jewish evidence for this angelic background can be stated briefly. Visionary experience of God was an important element in Jewish religion. Examples of it include the divine appearance to Moses and others in Exodus 24 and the vision attributed to Micaiah-ben-Imlah in 1 Kgs 22.19, not to mention the theophanies of the prophets Isaiah (6.1-4) and Ezekiel (1.26-27). God is portrayed there as if he resembled a human being (in what is sometimes called an 'anthropomorphic' theology), although of course no Jewish writer thought about him *merely* as a human being. He was also characteristically held to be seated on his heavenly throne surrounded by the angels as his courtiers. The throne of God is sometimes known by its Hebrew name as the *merkabah*. It is to some degree true to say that Judaism of the post-biblical period was embarrassed by the suggestion that God could be seen and indeed that he had a body. Some apocalypses (of which Asc. Isa. 9.37-38 is an example) deny that he could be seen in the context of an apocalyptic vision although other texts are more open about this. Medieval Judaism, however, rediscovered an interest in the body of God and engaged in considerable speculation about its proportions (the so-called *Shi'ur Qomah* literature; see Gruenwald 1980: 213-17).

Several Jewish writers describe an angel's appearance in terms modelled on the theophany. In the early second century BCE, before the book of Daniel was written, Ezekiel the Tragedian wrote a poem called the *Exagoge* in which he described how Moses ascended to heaven and took God's place on his throne, where he exercised a delegated authority as the deity became radically transcendent (see Hurtado 1988: 57-59). Ezekiel the Tragedian was followed by a number of writers, not the least of whom was the author of Daniel. Dan. 10.5-6 describes an angelophany in which the angel's appearance incorporates elements from the vision of God in Ezek. 1.26-27. The lightning, fire and bronze in Daniel 10 all derive from the description of God in that passage. This creates the impression that the angel is portrayed in quasi-divine terms as an exalted being among the heavenly host (see Rowland 1985). At Qumran Melchizedek was presented as a heavenly vizier called 'Elohim' in an interpretation of Psalm 82 (11QMelch; see Hurtado 1988: 78-79) while the Prayer of Joseph, which is preserved by Origen in his *Commentary on John* (2.31), calls the angel Israel the 'chief captain of the heavenly host' (see Smith 1985). The effect of this material, which is only a representative selection of the evidence that might be adduced, was to associate an angel with God in a way that distinguished him from other heavenly beings (see further Rowland 1982: 94-113). The fact that his appearance embodied elements from the theophany emphasized his unique position among the angels although this angel was never accorded worship in Judaism. Such angelology was an important aspect of Jewish mediatorial beliefs before the Christian period.

Some Christian writers took up this strand of angelology and used it to construct their descriptions of Jesus, even though Jesus was universally regarded as transcending the angels in early Christianity. Rev. 1.13-14 describes a vision of the heavenly Christ in language which borrows extensively from Dan. 10.5-6 (see Rowland 1980). The transfiguration story (Mk 9 and parallels) similarly uses angelophanic language to present the transformed Jesus as a heavenly being. Justin Martyr more than once called Christ an 'angel', among other titles (*Dial.* 61; 128), and he identified him in this way with the Angel of the Lord who appears on many occasions in the Pentateuch. Hermas thought of the Son of God as an enormous angel (e.g. Herm. Sim. 8.1-2) though he acknowledged that the Son was divine. While a real 'angel Christology' (the presentation of Christ quite literally as an angel) was a feature only of marginal groups like the Elkesaites, 'angelomorphic christology' of this broader kind is found in many of the New Testament writings and in later literature. It must not be regarded as peripheral; rather, in company with the Jewish Wisdom tradition it allowed some writers to present Jesus as akin and yet subordinate to God.

Angelomorphic christology is an important feature of the Ascension of Isaiah. The apocalypse presents the Beloved One as a glorious being in the seventh heaven who received angels' worship (9.27-28) but who also himself worshipped God (9.40-42). The Beloved's offering of worship is an indication that he shared the angels' duties in this respect. Two passages noted in the commentary particularly show the influence of Jewish angelology on the christology. Asc. Isa. 7.7-8 promises the prophet a vision of two divine powers, both of them greater than Isaiah's companion angel, in a context where the angel describes the Beloved as 'one greater than me'. This suggests that a comparison between the Beloved One and the angels was felt appropriate. The form of words used in 9.27 confirms that the author thought about the Beloved One in angelomorphic terms: 'And I saw one standing [there] whose glory surpassed that of all, and his glory was great and wonderful'. This description makes the Beloved the most glorious being in the seventh heaven (apart from God) but again uses language which involves a comparison with the angels. The Slavonic translation of the apocalypse (supported by L2) carefully removed this comparison: 'I turned to see the Lord who had great glory'. The Latin and Slavonic translations also transfer the words 'whose glory surpassed that of all' from the description of the Beloved One in 9.27 to a description of Michael which they have introduced in 9.23 (cf. their versions of 9.29, 42). The fact that these later translations apparently alter the text is a good indication of the angelomorphic basis of the original christology preserved in the Ethiopic translation. The text underlying the Ethiopic was from a period that had not experienced difficulties with this view which it seems to have been a characteristic mode of expression for the author of the Ascension of Isaiah.

Such angelomorphic language represents a way of describing the existence of more than one divinity which did not compromise the ultimate authority of God. Early Christianity apparently felt the need to preserve a form of monotheism despite the fact that Jesus was worshipped as divine. This is illustrated by 1 Cor. 8.6, where Paul describes Christian belief as belief in 'one God and one Lord' rather than in two Gods; the New Testament writings are somewhat reluctant to call Jesus 'God' at all (Jn 20.28 is an exception to this). The impetus towards Christian use of this Jewish angel strand lay in the fact that pre-Christian Judaism had already used theophanic language to describe the angel's mediation. This presentation of the mediator in divine terms was developed in Christian circles through the conviction that Jesus shared the divine *worship* (see Phil. 2.9-11), which no Jewish figure had done (cf. Asc. Isa. 7.17). A lingering feature of this angelomorphic influence in the Ascension of Isaiah is the fact that the apocalypse does not make the Beloved God's equal in every respect. This is shown both by his worship of God in 9.40-42 and also by his obedient response to God's command to descend in ch. 10, both of which presuppose that the mediator was subordinate to God.

The description of the Beloved's descent is modelled on an angelophany. As opposed to much New Testament 'sending' language, which describes the ministry of Jesus in metaphorical terms (e.g. Rom. 8.3; Gal. 4.4; Jn 3.14 and 1 Tim. 1.15 by contrast imply a prior existence in heaven), the Ascension of Isaiah presents a mythological drama which describes the commission and descent of a divine being into the world,

4. *The Ascension of Isaiah and Themes in Early Christianity* 83

his appearance there as a human person, and his subsequent return to heaven. Descent and ascension are briefly mentioned in John's Gospel (Jn 3.13; 6.62) but the Ascension of Isaiah attempts a more systematic explanation of the cause and nature of the descent than John or other first-century writers had offered. The author of the Ascension of Isaiah developed earlier christology by presenting the Beloved's commission as a heavenly event (10.6-17) and by introducing the language of 'transformation into human likeness' (3.13) to explain his earthly appearance. These were new features in the christological tradition, and they came in part to determine the way in which subsequent writers spoke about the mission of the Son of God.

A number of stories in the Pentateuch describe how a heavenly being appeared to people as a human person. This is said about the angels who greeted Abraham in Genesis 18 (three men are mentioned by Gen. 18.2) and about the angel who announced the birth of Samson in Judges 13 (he is repeatedly said to be a man by that chapter, although he is also said to have a 'terrible countenance' biblical). With these texts should be compared the description of Raphael's activity in the book of Tobit (chs. 3-12; the identification of Jacob with the angel Israel in the Prayer of Joseph mentioned already in this Guide; and the appearance of Michael in the Testament of Abraham, who is described there as a 'most handsome soldier' (2.2-4). All these texts maintain that a heavenly being could temporarily acquire human form when appearing on earth.

In many ways it is Tobit which best illustrates how Jewish writers understood an angelophany. The description of Raphael's activity occupies a substantial part of that work. Tobit describes how Raphael was commissioned in heaven by God (3.16-17), how the angel appeared to Tobias apparently as a human person (5.4-5), the revelation of his identity once his mission was complete (12.15), and his ascension back to heaven (12.20). The last two of these seem to be related events. A further element in Tobit is the denial that the mediator needed food or drink when on earth (12.19).

There are signs that an angelophany of this kind influenced the author of the Ascension of Isaiah. As in Tobit the Beloved's mission is said to have begun with a heavenly commission by God (10.6-17). Tobit does not describe Raphael's descent but this is certainly presupposed by 5.3-4, which finds the angel on earth in human form. In a similar way the Ascension of Isaiah makes the point that the human Jesus is the form which the Beloved One adopted when he appeared on earth; his descent into the womb of Mary (ch. 11) and transformation into human likeness (3.13) are significant elements in the apocalypse. The traditions about Jesus are inserted into the context of the mediator's descent in 3.13-18 and 11.2-22 and were originally separate from it. Asc. Isa. 11.17 furthermore hints that the Beloved did not really need human food in its description of the suckling. This perhaps reflects the influence of the view found in Tob. 12.19, although the hint is merely a passing one in the Ascension of Isaiah. The Ascension of Isaiah also draws a connection between the Beloved's revelation of his identity and the moment of his departure from earth by explaining that the mediator was first recognized by angels in the firmament (11.23-24). This recalls the conclusion of Tobit's angelophany, where the angel ascended to heaven after explaining who he was.

It is not necessary to suppose that the author of the Ascension of Isaiah modelled his christology specifically on Tobit (although he may have known the text). He seems rather to have been aware of the angelophanic pattern found in Tobit and in other literature and to have drawn on it for his description of the Beloved One. The notion of the Beloved's appearance in human form thus preserved an idea about the advent of a heavenly messenger which had circulated in Jewish literature for centuries. The angelophany allowed this Christian writer to describe the appearance of the heavenly mediator as the human Jesus, which is the kind of belief that the christological tradition was coming to require given its conviction that Jesus was connected with the divine presence (cf. Jn 1.14; 18). In this way he offered a theory about how the ministry of Jesus was connected with events in the heavenly world by describing the commission and descent of a heavenly mediator.

The christology of the Ascension of Isaiah thus makes use of more than one angelological strand to describe the Beloved One's activity. Behind the view of the Beloved as the divine subordinate stands a history of reflection in Judaism in which an angel was described in language drawn from the theophany. The descent myth draws on the angelophany to describe the mediator's appearance as Jesus. The author did this within a religious context which recognized that Jesus was divine and not simply an angel. Such use of angelology was an important way in which early Christianity developed its beliefs about Jesus.

4. *The Ascension of Isaiah and Themes in Early Christianity* 85

Docetism

A further feature of the Ascension of Isaiah is its tendency to assume that Jesus had superhuman abilities. This is a consequence of the view that he was the temporary appearance of the Beloved One who had come from heaven. The name generally given to this kind of christology is 'docetism'. Docetism denotes a view of Jesus, judged unorthodox by mainstream Christian writers in the second century, which devalued or detracted from his humanity by drawing attention to the divine element which gave him extraordinary powers. The term denotes a complex of beliefs in Christian antiquity rather than a single, coherent point of view. It surfaces in a mild form in the Ascension of Isaiah but other sources are less cautious in discussing the extraordinary abilities of Jesus.

The description of these other forms helps to explain the nature of the docetism in the Ascension of Isaiah. Ignatius knew of people who taught that Jesus only *seemed* to suffer, against whom he asserted the reality of the Saviour's birth, life and suffering (Ign. Trall. 9.1-2). The Asian heretic Cerinthus taught that Christ was a heavenly mediator who descended on Jesus at his baptism and returned to heaven before the crucifixion (according to Irenaeus, *Adv. Haer.* 1.26). The Gnostic Basileides believed that Jesus and Simon of Cyrene changed forms on the way to the cross so that Simon was crucified at Calvary and Jesus mocked those who thought that they had killed him (according to Irenaeus, *Adv. Haer.* 1.24). These three examples hold in common the belief that Christ did not really die on the cross, although Cerinthus acknowledged that *Jesus* did so. They represent an attempt to distinguish Jesus from Christ in a way which allowed the superhuman properties of the mediator to qualify a normal understanding of the humanity of Jesus.

The Ascension of Isaiah must be distinguished from these kinds of docetism because its author insists that the Beloved One was really born of Mary and that he truly died on the cross (3.13; 9.26; 11.19-20). The author would have agreed with Ignatius in this, whatever other differences existed between them. The docetism found in the apocalypse is a mild form which accepts the possibility of an abnormal pregnancy (11.7-8) and questions whether the infant really needed Mary's suckling (11.17) but which does not allow the inclusion of the mediatorial pattern to deny the reality of the Beloved One's birth and death. This mild docetism retains the tensions between human person and heavenly mediator inherited from the Jewish angelophanic background. The Ascension of Isaiah has much to say about the way in which the person of Jesus was understood in second-century Christianity. It represents a stage of belief in which it was recognized that Jesus' ministry had begun and ended in heaven, but where the precise relationship between the heavenly and human aspects had yet to be fully defined.

Eschatology

The work's eschatology also calls for comment. The Ascension of Isaiah includes more than one eschatological view. The early chapters (1–5) contain the hope that the Beloved would return from heaven to establish his earthly kingdom. Chapters 6–11 lack any formal articulation of this future hope and concentrate instead on the Beloved's victory over Beliar and his heavenly enthronement as evidence that salvation had been fully provided. It is difficult now to decide how far these views were intended by their author to cohere with each other.

The eschatology of the early chapters is a millenarian one. The term 'millenarianism' is generally defined by citing Rev. 20.4, a passage which expects that Christian martyrs would reign with Christ on earth for a thousand years. The author of Revelation was at one with other first-century writers in this future hope even if his timescale for the future reign is more precise than is found elsewhere. Paul also expected that the living and dead would reign with the messiah on earth (cf. 1 Thess. 4.13-18; 1 Cor. 6.2-3; 15.24-28). Many second- and third-century writers developed this view, often by exegesis of the book of Revelation (see Bietenhard 1953). The author of the Ascension of Isaiah thus stood within a tradition of Christian eschatology when he wrote 4.14-18. His distinctive contribution to that tradition was to introduce the timescale from Dan. 12.12 in 4.12, 14. This represents an attempt to specify the time when the *parousia* would occur with a precision that other Christian writers generally avoided.

The progress of thought in the apocalypse suggests that chs. 6–11 were written with the intention of supplementing rather than criticizing the eschatology of 4.14-18. The second half of the Ascension of Isaiah gives no sign that a different situation was addressed and indeed are reasons for supposing that the apocalypse was written with a consistent purpose in mind. The two halves of the work evidently offer different perspectives on the same situation. The Second Vision, like the First, was written to create hope. The author does this by constructing an ideal state at variance with reality in which his apocalyptic interest allowed the disclosure that the Beloved One had defeated Beliar on the cross. This assured readers that their heavenly patron was more powerful than the demon who inspired the Romans and that Beliar had been defeated despite what Rome was doing in the world, so that a new perspective was possible.

The author's purpose in the Second Vision was to change readers' response to their situation by constructing a picture of how salvation had emerged from cosmic disorder. We might call this a 'utopian' perspective. Utopianism denotes the construction of an ideal state that is intended to bring about a change in present conditions (see Mannheim 1991: 173). Both the description of the cross as the moment of salvation and the image of the Beloved's enthronement offered readers a new way of looking at their situation which supplied hope by insisting that *their* patron reigned supreme. In a world in which people believed in gods and demons, and in which Christians found themselves at the mercy of the Roman government, this author claimed that the Beloved One had decisively defeated the inferior powers who stood behind the Roman adversaries. Readers were thereby encouraged to trust the Beloved One at this time of difficulty in their lives. This material does not however mask the *actual* nature of the situation, which is described in ch. 4.

It is certainly mistaken to underestimate the realism with which the primitive Christians held their *parousia* hopes, but the question arises of whether the Second Vision does not qualify the millenarian eschatology of Asc. Isa. 4.14-18. This is because it juxtaposes more ambivalent material with the formal prediction of the *parousia*. As time wore on the material may have suggested a way of coping with the increasing sense of disappointment with *parousia* hopes by advocating trust in what the Beloved had already accomplished rather than in what he might do in the future. The timeless nature of chs. 6–11 does much to explain the Ascension of Isaiah's popularity in later Christianity where its portrait of the heavenly Christ was especially valued. This utopian image of the Beloved One's victory over Beliar is an early example of the way in which Christianity began to transform its millenarian basis by constructing a more systematic complex of beliefs in which christology stood to the fore and where what had happened in the past, rather than the hope for future divine intervention, was made the critical factor.

Mariology

A further reason for interest in the Ascension of Isaiah is the nature of the work's beliefs about Mary. Chapter 11 of the Ethiopic text presents her, like Joseph, as a Davidide. This agrees with information found in Prot. Jas 10.1; Ign. Eph. 18.2; and Justin, *Dial.* 45.4. Her Davidic descent is not mentioned in the New Testament writings, however. It is virtually impossible to comment on the historicity of this report in the Ascension of Isaiah and other sources, except to note that the idea is not found in writings earlier than the second century and that it might easily have been created in the interests of reinforcing Jesus' messianic status. On the other hand it would have been natural for Joseph to marry someone from his own tribe, so that the information might conceivably have been omitted by Matthew and Luke for reasons known best to themselves. The issue remains a finely-balanced one and it is consequently difficult to resolve.

The Ascension of Isaiah provides early evidence for the belief that Mary remained a virgin following the birth of Jesus (11.9). This idea was repeated in the later Protevangelium of James (c. 150 CE), which said that Mary's birth, like Jesus', was divinely ordained. In the third century the Alexandrian scholar Origen would assert that Mary remained *perpetually* a virgin (*Hom. in Luc.* 7.4) and that Jesus' brothers mentioned by the Gospel were Joseph's children by another woman (for the last point cf. Prot. Jas 9.2). This issue was one that prompted a considerable discussion in the ancient Christian world.

Cosmology

The Ascension of Isaiah is exceptional among early Christian writings in presenting a seven-storied cosmology (see Gruenwald 1980: 57-62). This view is found in Jewish apocalyptic and rabbinic writings (e.g. *b. Hag.* 12b), but Paul alone of the New Testament writers explicitly acknowledges more than one heaven (he mentions three in 2 Cor. 12.2). The book of Revelation and Hermas, two early Christian apocalyptic texts, mention only one heaven, as do John's Gospel and Hebrews. Perhaps this reluctance to speak of more than one heaven depends on the conviction held by all primitive Christians that God was an accessible deity who had been revealed by Jesus; but Paul's mystical allusion in 2 Corinthians 12 is suggestive of a more speculative interest in at least some circles of the emerging religion.

4. The Ascension of Isaiah and Themes in Early Christianity 89

A whole variety of Jewish texts show that belief in a diversity of heavens was an important feature of the apocalyptic interest (for discussion of these see Gruenwald 1980: 29-72). The author of the Ascension of Isaiah used this view to emphasize the distinction between the Beloved One and Beliar with its soteriological implications. The distinctive feature of his cosmology is the fact that Beliar was excluded from even the lowest heaven and confined to the firmament. This is a development from the cosmology of passages such as Eph. 2.2; 6.12, where demonic powers hostile to Christians were located 'in the air'. The cosmology of the Ascension of Isaiah supports a profoundly transcendent theology in which God was an enthroned deity in the seventh heaven; but this perspective is qualified through the fact that the Beloved as the divine subordinate descended to earth so that the human Jesus embodied a mediator who had come from the presence of God.

The work's cosmology is distinctive for another reason as well. The author models the angelic arrangement of the lower heavens on the vision of the three seated divinities with which the apocalypse concludes (11.32-33), so that the cosmology is reminiscent of the Trinitarian theology in its structure. This was apparently connected with the attempt to explain how Christian faith was superior to the worship of Beliar, in which the arrangement of even the lower heavens emphasized their difference from the firmament and thus the demon's inferior position. The notion that each heaven contained a *merkabah* was preserved in the later writing called the Visions of Ezekiel (see Gruenwald 1980: 134-41), but otherwise it did not exercise a great effect on subsequent literature.

The Ascension of Isaiah and Gnosticism

An aspect of interpretation which has caused interest in the past is the relationship between the Ascension of Isaiah and Gnosticism. 'Gnosticism' is the name given to a complex of religions which flourished from about the middle of the CE and which taught that there had been strife amongst the heavenly beings (aeons) as a result of which the world was created (for an introduction see Rudolph 1983). Gnosticism presented human beings as fallen light-particles imprisoned in bodies. Gnostic initiates had been alerted to their condition by the illumination disclosed by the Redeemer, who descended to earth in the mythology expounded by some of the Gnostic systems. The Gnostics' aim was to secure repatriation with the heavenly world after death by learning a complicated system of passwords which would enable the ascending soul to avoid the traps set for it by the warders who guarded the individual heavens.

The Ascension of Isaiah has sometimes been presented as a Gnostic apocalypse because it incorporates a number of themes which surface in the later Gnostic literature. Examples of this include the notion of heavenly warders and the sequence of passwords in ch. 10, the words 'We alone are' (10.12; cf. the 'I am the Lord' of 4.6) which would later be spoken by the Gnostic Demiurge in the Apocryphon of John, and the theme of Beloved's descent which has sometimes been compared with the descent of the Gnostic 'Redeemer' (as by Helmbold 1972).

It is important to make the point that the Ascension of Isaiah cannot be considered a Gnostic writing in the true sense. In the first place matters of dating tell against this suggestion. The Ascension of Isaiah was written before 138 CE but the earliest Gnostic apocalypse was not written before about 150 CE. There are also some significant differences between the Ascension of Isaiah and Gnosticism. For example, Beliar is excluded from the heavens in the Ascension of Isaiah but Gnostic literature made the Demiurge, the jealous creator of the human world, a member of the aeonic system. This represents a more complex cosmic dualism than that found in the Ascension of Isaiah. Moreover, Asc. Isa. 7.9-12 takes no interest in cosmogony, whereas cosmogony (of a complex mythological kind) lay at the heart of Gnosticism with its teaching about the Demiurge (whom some sources even identified with the Jewish God). The Ascension of Isaiah says that Beliar and his angels had been striving *since* creation (7.12), not that their strife was the cause of creation, which was the view adopted in Gnostic cosmogony. Nor does the Ascension of Isaiah share the Gnostic pessimism about human life; Isaiah was instructed to return to his flesh (11.35), a command which Gnostics would have abhorred.

The Ascension of Isaiah is thus better explained as a Jewish-Christian apocalyptic writing, perhaps a unique kind of text, than as an early Gnostic apocalypse. Its differences from Gnosticism must be acknowledged quite as much as the similarities are affirmed. The Ascension of Isaiah nevertheless provides an important link between the New Testament and Gnosticism since it shows how a cosmological and mediatorial interest was developed by Christians in the early second century CE.

Concluding Remarks

This Guide has presented the Ascension of Isaiah as a Jewish-Christian apocalypse which was written in the early second century CE and which reveals much about the nature of Christianity at that time. It specifically addresses a difficult period in the history of relations between the Christians and the Roman government, when Roman imposition of the sacrifice test had been recognized to constitute a problem. The apocalypse was written to create hope in his situation. The author achieved this purpose by offering a millenarian and then a utopian eschatology which showed that Beliar was subordinate to the Beloved One. In these ways the Ascension of Isaiah encouraged readers who had reason to fear Rome's power over their lives. Soteriology is an important concern in the Ascension of Isaiah and this explains the prominence of christology there.

The difficulties of interpreting the Ascension of Isaiah are compounded by the absence of a reliable edition of the text, although this problem will be solved when the Italian edition appears. Many aspects of interpretation remain provisional given the lack of agreement in the past over when the apocalypse was written and the dearth of research which it has received. Nevertheless it is generally agreed that the Ascension of Isaiah contains valuable insights for the study of christology, eschatology and early Christian social history, quite apart from the intruiging question of its relation with the New Testament literature. The Ascension of Isaiah must feature in further study of all these areas. The next decade will doubtless reveal what it has to contribute to them and will no doubt also witness a resurgence of interest in the apocalypse itself when the new edition places its text on a surer footing.

Further Reading

Christology
There are a number of standard treatments of New Testament Christology. These include Dunn 1980; Cullmann 1959; Fuller 1979; Hahn 1979; and de Jonge 1988.

Millenarianism
Millenarianism is the belief that the returning Christ would inaugurate an earthly kingdom. There are studies of this aspect of Christian belief by Bietenhard (1953) and Daniélou (1964: 377-404). One of the more interesting

aspects of modern research is the recognition that cultural anthropology can illuminate primitive Christian eschatology. Two studies often cited in this connection are Burridge 1969 and Worsley 1957.

Mariology
The issues surrounding the birth of Jesus are examined by Brown (1993) See also Graef 1963, 1965 and Brown (ed.), Donfried, Fitzmyer and Reumann 1978.

Gnosticism
Gnosticism was a complex of religious beliefs that flourished from about the middle of the second century CE onwards. There are introductions to it by Rudolph (1983) and Grant (1966). There is an important volume of essays on the subject edited by Hedrick and Hodgson (1986). The Gnostic library discovered at Nag Hammadi has been translated under the editorship of Robinson (1988).

General Bibliography

Aune, D.E
    1983   *Prophecy in Early Christianity and the Ancient Mediterranean World* (Grand Rapids: Eerdmans).

Bauckham, R.J.
    1980–81   'The Worship of Jesus in Apocalyptic Christianity', *NTS* 27: 322-41.

Bauer, W.
    1972   *Orthodoxy and Heresy in Earliest Christianity* (ET; London: SCM Press).

Bietenhard, H.
    1953   'The Millenial Hope in the Early Church', *SJT* 6: 12-30.

Bori, P.C.
    1980   'L'estasi del profeta: Ascensio Isaiae 6 el'Antico Profetismo Cristiano', *Cristianesimo nella' Storia* 1: 367-89.
    1983   'L'esperienza profetica nell'Ascensione di Isaia', in Pesce (ed.) 1983: 133-54.

Brown, R.E.
    1993   *The Birth of the Messiah* (New York: Doubleday, 2nd edn).

Brown, R.E., K.P. Donfried, J.A. Fitzmyer and J. Reumann (eds.)
    1978   *Mary in the New Testament* (Philadelphia: Fortress Press).

Burridge, K.
    1969   *New Heaven, New Earth* (Oxford: Basil Blackwell).

Chadwick, H.
    1967   *The Early Church* (Harmondsworth: Penguin Books).

Charles, R.H.
    1900   *The Ascension of Isaiah* (London: A. & C. Black).

Charlesworth, J.H.
    1981   'Christian and Jewish Self-Definition in Light of the Christian Additions to the Apocryphal Writings', in E.P. Sanders (ed.), *Jewish and Christian Self-Definition* (London): II, 41-46.

Charlesworth, J.H. (ed.)
    1983, 1985   *The Old Testament Pseudepigrapha* (2 vols.; London: Doubleday).

Caquot, A.
    1973   'Bref Commentaire du Martyre d'Isaie', *Semitica* 23 65-93.

Collins, J.J.
    1974   *The Sibylline Oracles of Egyptian Judaism* (SBLDS, 13; Missoula, MT: Scholars Press).

1977 *The Apocalyptic Vision of the Book of Daniel* (Missoula, MT: Scholars Press).
1983 *The Sibylline Oracles*, in Charlesworth (ed.) 1983: 317-472.
Collins, J.J.(ed.)
1979 'Apocalypse: The Morphology of a Genre', *Semeia* 14.
Collins, A.Y.
1984 *Crisis and Catharsis: The Power of the Apocalypse* (Philadelphia: Westminster Press).
Cullmann, O.
1963 *The Christology of the New Testament* (ET; London: SCM Press, 2nd edn).
Daniélou, J.
1964 *The Theology of Jewish Christianity* (ET; London: SCM Press).
De Jonge, M.
1988 *Christology in Context, the Earliest Christian Response to Jesus* (Philadelphia: Westminster Press).
De Ste Croix, G.E.M.
1963 'Why Were the Early Christians Persecuted?', *Past and Present* 24: 26-38.
Dunn, J.D.G.
1980 *Christology in the Making* (London: SCM Press).
1990 *Unity and Diversity in the New Testament* (London: SCM Press).
Flusser, D.
1953 'The Apocryphal Book of *Ascensio Isaiae* and the Dead Sea Sect', *IEJ* 3: 30-47.
Frend, W.H.C.
1965 *Martyrdom and Persecution in the Early Church* (Oxford: Basil Blackwell).
1986 *The Rise of Christianity* (London: Darton, Longman and Todd).
1991 *The Early Church: From the Beginnings to 461* (London: SCM Press, 3rd edn).
Friedrich, G.
1983 'Prophets in the Early Church', *TDNT* VI: 856-61.
Fuller, R.
1979 *The Foundations of New Testament Christology* (London: Fount Paperbacks).
Gager, J.G
1983 *The Origins of Anti-semitism: Attitudes towards Judaism in Pagan and Christian Antiquity* (Oxford: Oxford University Press).
Graef, H.C.
1963, 1965 *Mary: A History of Doctrine and Devotion* (2 vols.; London and New York: Sheed and Ward).

Grant, R.M.
  1966   *Gnosticism and Early Christianity* (New York: Columbia University Press, 2nd edn).
Gruenwald, I.
  1980   *Apocalyptic and Merkabah Mysticism* (Leiden: Brill).
Hall, R.G.
  1990   '*The Ascension of Isaiah*: Community Situation, Date, and Place in Early Christianity', *JBL* 109.2: 289-306.
Hahn, F.
  1969   *The Titles of Jesus in Christology: Their History in Early Christianity* (London: Lutterworth).
Hanson, P.D.
  1979   *The Dawn of Apocalyptic* (Philadelphia: Fortress Press).
Hedrick, C.W., and R. Hodgson
  1986   *Nag Hammadi, Gnosticism and Early Christianity* (Peabody: Hendrickson).
Helmbold, A.K.
  1972   'Gnostic Elements in the Ascension of Isaiah', *NTS* 18: 222-27.
Hill, D.
  1979   *New Testament Prophecy* (London: Marshall, Morgan and Scott).
Hurtado, L.W.
  1988   *One God, One Lord* (London: SCM Press).
Jeffers, J.S.
  1991   *Conflict at Rome: Social Order and Hierarchy in Early Christianity* (Minneapolis: Fortress Press).
Knibb, M.A.
  1985   *The Ascension of Isaiah* in Charlesworth (ed.) 1985: 143-76.
Klijn, A.F.J., and G. Reininck
  1973   *Patristic Evidence for Jewish-Christian Sects* (NTSup 36; Leiden: Brill).
Lampe, G.W.
  1984   'AD 70 in Christian Reflection', in C.F.D. Moule and E. Bammel (eds.), *Jesus and the Politics of his Day* (Cambridge: Cambridge University Press), 153-71.
Larkin, K.J.
  1994   *The Eschatology of Second Zechariah: A Study of the Formation of a Mantological Wisdom Anthology* (Kampen: Kok Pharos Press).
Longenecker, R.N.
  1970   *The Christology of Early Jewish Christianity* (London: SCM Press).
MacMullen, R.
  1981   *Paganism in the Roman Empire* (New Haven and London: Yale University Press).
  1984   *Christianizing the Roman Empire (AD 100-400)* (New York: Yale University Press).

Mannheim, K.
1991   Ideology and Utopia: An Introduction to the Sociology of Knowledge (ET; London: Routledge, new edn).

Markus, R.A.
1974   Christianity in the Roman World (London: Thames and Hudson).

Metzger, B.M.
1977   The Early Versions of the New Testament (Oxford: Oxford University Press).

Pesce, M.
1983   'Presupposti per l'utilazzione storica dell' Ascensione di Isaia: Formazione e tradizione del testo; genere letterario; cosmologia angelica', in Pesce (ed.) 1983: 13-76.

Pesce, M. (ed.)
1983   Isaia, il Diletto e la Chiesa (Brescia: Paideia).

Robinson, J.M.
1988   The Nag Hammadi Library in English (Leiden: Brill, 3rd edn).

Rowland, C.C.
1980   'The Vision of the Risen Christ in Rev. 1, 13ff.: The Debt of an Early Christology to an Aspect of Jewish Angelology', JTS 31: 1-11.
1982   The Open Heaven (London: SPCK).
1985   'A Man Clothed in Linen: Daniel 10.6ff. and Jewish Angelology', JSNT 24: 99-110.

Rudolph, K.
1983   Gnosis: The Nature and History of an Ancient Religion (ET; Edinburgh: T. & T. Clark).

Russell, D.S.
1964   The Method and Message of Jewish Apocalyptic (London: SCM Press).

Schoedel, W.R.
1985   Ignatius of Antioch (Philadelphia: Fortress Press).

Smith, J.Z.
1985   The Prayer of Joseph in Charlesworth (ed.) 1985: 699-714.

Staniforth, M.
1987   Early Christian Writings: The Apostolic Fathers (Harmondsworth: Penguin Books).

Stevenson, J.
1987   A New Eusebius (London: SPCK, rev. edn).

Stone, M.E.
1976   'Lists of Revealed Things in the Apocalyptic Literature', in F.M. Cross (ed.), Magnalia Dei: The Mighty Acts of God (New York: Doubleday): 414-54.

Thiele, E.R.
1983   The Mysterious Numbers of the Hebrew Kings (Grand Rapids: Zondervan, 3rd edn).

Thompson, L.
  1990   *The Book of Revelation, Apocalypse and Empire* (Oxford: Oxford University Press).
Ullendorff, E.
  1968   *Ethiopia and the Bible* (London: Oxford University Press).
Worsley, P.
  1957   *The Trumpet shall Sound* (London: MacGibbon and Kee).

INDEXES

INDEX OF REFERENCES

OLD TESTAMENT

Genesis		2 Chronicles		34	31, 57
18	83	33.11	52		
18.2	83			Daniel	
19	53	Psalms		10	80
		45	49	10.2-3	51
Exodus		82	80	10.5-6	80, 81
24	80	110.1	77	12.2	63
33.20	28, 29, 52			12.12	61, 86
		Isaiah			
Deuteronomy		1.10	53	Zechariah	
18.10-11	50	6	9	14.5	62
19.15	47	6.1-7	55		
21.22-23	30	6.1-4	28, 77, 80	Tobit	
		6.1	52	3–12	83
Judges		7.3	48	3.16-17	83
13	83	13	9, 64	5.3-4	83
		37.32	62	5.4-5	83
1 Kings		38	49	12.15	83
17.2	62	45	60, 61	12.19	83, 84
22.19	51, 55, 80	45.18	18, 60	12.20	83
22.24	51	52.13–53.12	64		
				1 Maccabees	
2 Kings		Ezekiel		2.28-30	62
1	51	1	67	4.46	33
18–20	49	1.26-27	80		

NEW TESTAMENT

Matthew		27.62-66	54	10.18	60
3.1-12	62			19.43-44	30
8.20	34	Mark		21.20-24	30
20.22	65	9	81	24.4	54
26.39	65			24.50-52	76
27.25	30, 54	Luke			
		10.8-12	34		

Index of References

John		10.4	29	2 Thessalonians	
1.14	84	10.11	77	1.6-7	63
1.18	84	11.5-10	35	1.7	62
3.13	16, 37, 54, 71	11.5	35	2.1-10	60
		12–14	13, 35	2.9-10	61
3.14	82, 83	12.28	34-36		
6.62	16, 55, 83	14.1-5	35, 36	1 Timothy	
7.27-28	75	15.24-28	63, 86	1.15	82
12.31	48	15.24-25	12, 49		
14.28	73			1 Peter	
14.30	48	2 Corinthians		2.13	43
16.11	48	4.4	48	2.17	43
19.1-16	30	12	19, 88	3.22	48, 76, 77
20.12-13	54	12.2	88		
20.28	82			2 Peter	
		Galatians		2.1-22	57
Acts		3.13	30	3.4-7	56
1.9-11	76	4.4	82	3 1	31
7.55	65				
8.1-3	30	Ephesians		Revelation	
9.8	67	2.2	89	1.13-14	81
11.27-28	34	2.20	36	2.13	18, 22
14.12	39	6.12	89	4.1	67
17.5	30			12.6	62
21.38	62	Philippians		12.9	60
24	38	2.5-11	54	12.14	62
		2.9-11	74, 82	13	60
Romans				17	60
8.3	82	Colossians		19.10	70
8.34	77	2.15	20, 48, 74	20.4	12, 86
13	43			20.5	63
		1 Thessalonians		21	64
1 Corinthians		2.14-16	30	22.8-9	70
2.8	71, 76	3.13	62		
6.2-3	86	4.13-18	86		
8.6	30, 49, 73, 82				

PSEUDEPIGRAPHA

Asc. Isa.		1.7-9	14	2.1	14, 64
1–5	10, 25, 86	1.7-8	85	2.2	49
1	23	1.7	49	2.3-4	50
1.1–3.12	10	1.9	49	2.4–4.4	23
1.1-6	14	1.10	49	2.4	50
1.1	23, 47	1.11	49	2.7-11	10, 13, 16, 32, 36, 37, 42, 48, 62, 65, 67
1.2	47	1.13	49		
1.3	48, 77	2–5	23		
1.4	49	2	14, 49, 58		

2.7-8	14		51, 57, 58,			32, 43, 44,
2.7	50, 58		66, 67			53, 62, 63,
2.8	50	3.21-22	23			86, 87
2.9-11	14	3.21	15, 16, 21,	4.14		18, 48, 56,
2.9	48, 50, 58,		31, 33, 50,			57, 62, 86
	67		56	4.15		18, 63
2.10	51	3.23	57	4.16		18, 63
2.11	51	3.24	16, 31, 57	4.17		18, 44, 63,
2.12-16	51	3.25	16, 42, 56,			70
2.12-13	51		57	4.18		18, 57, 63,
2.12	51	3.26-28	16, 56			64
2.13	51	3.26-27	10, 67	4.19		64
2.14–3.13	24	3.26	16, 31, 36,	4.20		32, 64
2.14-16	51		58	4.21-22		28, 29, 48,
2.14	51	3.27-28	13, 16, 31			53, 64
3	15, 49, 50	3.27	58, 62	4.21		64
3.1	52	3.28	37, 58	5		11, 14, 18,
3.6-12	52	3.29	58			21, 22, 38,
3.6-10	28	3.30	58			42, 43, 49,
3.6	15, 52, 53	3.31	9, 10, 13, 16,			51, 58, 64,
3.7	52		31-33, 36,			66
3.8-10	15, 28, 52,		45, 57, 58	5.1-16		10
	53, 64	4	11, 18, 19,	5.1		64
3.9-10	28		22, 38, 42,	5.2		65
3.10	15, 53		44, 48, 57,	5.3-6		65
3.11	53		59-61, 64,	5.7		65
3.12	15, 53, 64		69, 87	5.8		65
3.13–4.22	10, 14, 26,	4.1-13	10, 15, 16,	5.9		65
	53		30-32, 38,	5.10		65
3.13-18	15, 20, 49,		45, 53	5.11-12		65
	53, 56, 75,		59	5.13		23, 35, 42,
	84	4.2	21, 40, 60			43, 62, 65
3.13	15, 16, 28,	4.3	19, 21, 42	5.14		65
	52-54, 70,	4.4	60	5.15-16		65
	83-85	4.5	18, 42, 60,	6–11		10-14, 22-
		4.6	61, 74, 90			26, 32, 43-
3.14	54		61			45, 86, 87
3.15	54	4.7-11	61	6		10, 14, 32,
3.16-17	54-56	4.7	18, 38, 42,			37, 66, 67
3.16	55	4.8	61	6.1		23, 47, 66
3.17-18	55		17, 50, 61	6.2		66
3.17	55	4.9	61	6.3		48, 66
3.18	16, 54, 55,	4.10	38, 42, 61	6.4		66
	72	4.11	61, 62, 86	6.5		66
3.19-20	15, 16, 53,	4.12	22, 35, 42,	6.6		67
	56	4.13	50, 61, 62,	6.7		67
3.21-31	10, 13, 15,		65	6.8		67
	16, 30-32,		10-12, 15,	6.9		67
	35, 37, 38,	4.14-18				

6.10	67	8.17	71	10.12	74, 90
6.11	67	8.25-28	71	10.13-14	20
6.12	67	9–11	79	10.13	60, 74
6.13	67	9	20, 69, 72	10.14-15	74
6.14-17	13	9.1	71	10.14	20, 55
6.14	32, 36, 58, 67	9.2	71, 72	10.17-31	54
		9.3	25	10.17-30	20
6.17	32, 36, 48, 58, 67	9.5	22, 23, 74	10.25	75
		9.6-7	71	10.29	75
7–11	19	9.8-9	71	10.30-31	75
7–9	19	9.12	71	11	20, 24, 75, 84, 88
7	19, 55, 69	9.13-17	71		
7.1-19	24	9.13	71	11.2-22	15, 20, 24, 25, 49, 56, 75, 84
7.1	68	9.14	71		
7.2	68	9.16	71, 76		
7.3-6	68	9.17-18	72	11.2	75
7.3	68	9.19-23	70, 72	11.3	75
7.7-8	24, 68, 81	9.23	73, 82	11.4	75
7.9-12	11, 19, 20, 48, 59, 68, 69, 90	9.24-26	55, 71, 72	11.5-6	75
		9.26	85	11.7-8	20
		9.27-42	72	11.8	75
7.9	68	9.27-36	20, 73	11.9	75, 88
7.10	19, 44, 68	9.27-28	81	11.10	75
7.11	69	9.27	81, 82	11.11	75
7.12	19, 69, 90	9.28	72	11.12	75
7.13	70	9.29	73, 82	11.13	75
7.14	70	9.30	72, 75	11.14	56, 75
7.15	70	9.32	72	11.16	76
7.17	49, 55, 70, 72, 82	9.33-36	73	11.17	20, 76, 84, 85
		9.33	73		
7.21	70	9.36	73	11.18	76
7.22	70	9.37-38	63, 71, 73, 80	11.19-20	20, 85
7.23	55			11.19	28, 76
7.24-27	70	9.39	73	11.20	76
7.24	70	9.40-42	20, 73, 81, 82	11.21	76
7.25	70			11.22-33	20
7.28	70	9.42	73, 82	11.22-23	76
7.32-37	70	10–11	19, 68, 80	11.22	76
7.37	70	10	20, 44, 55, 73, 74, 82, 90	11.23-33	11, 44, 48, 54, 77
8	19				
8.1	70			11.23-24	20, 76, 84
8.2	70	10.6-17	20, 48, 54, 83	11.24-25	76
8.5	70			11.32-33	19, 50, 52, 55, 73, 89
8.7	70	10.7-16	74		
8.9-10	70	10.7	22, 71	11.32	21, 45, 72, 77
8.11	71	10.8	63		
8.14-15	71	10.11	74	11.33	21, 77
8.16-28	71	10.12-13	69	11.34-35	77

11.35	71, 90	*1 Enoch*		12.51	51
11.36-43	77	14	55, 67		
11.37-38	21, 77	89.61-65	57	*Sib. Or.*	
11.39	77	89.68	31	3.63-74	17, 59
11.40	77	90.26	63	3.63-65	60
11.41	77			4.186	63
11.42-43	78	*2 Enoch*		5	59
		1.4	68	5.101-4	22, 59
2 Baruch				8.456-61	75
59.10	63	*4 Ezra*			
		7.36	63	*T. Abr.*	
		9.26	51	2.2-4	83

CHRISTIAN AUTHORS

1 Clem.		*Gosp. Pet.*		Irenaeus	
5.4	17, 40, 60	39	54	*Adv. Haer.*	
6.1-2	40			1.3.2	71
23.3-4	56	Hermas		1.24	85
30.1	58	*Man.*		1.26	85
42	36	2.3	58		
44	12, 36			Justin	
		Sim.		*1 Apol.*	
2 Clem.		8.1-2	81	47	30
4.3	58				
11.2-4	56	Hippolytus		*Dial.*	
		Dem. adv. Jud.		110	30
Did.		6–7	30	128	81
10.7	34			45.4	88
11	34	Ignatius		61	81
11.7	34	*Eph.*			
13	34	6.1	33	Origen	
13.1	34	18.2	88	*Comm. on John*	
13.2	34	19.1	76	2.31	80
13.3	34				
13.4	34	*Magn.*		*Contra Celsum*	
15.1	36, 57	6.1	33	1.47	30
Epistula Apostolorum		*Rom.*		*Hom. in Luc.*	
13–14	75	4.1	65, 66	7.4	88
		4.3	17, 40, 60		
Eusebius				*Prot. Jas*	
Hist Eccl.		*Trall.*		9.2	88
3.20	41	9.1-2	85	10.1	88

CLASSICAL AUTHORS

Dio Cassius		Pliny		Nero	
Epitome		*Ep.*		16.2	40
64.9	59	10.96-97	41		
67.14	40	10.96	11, 17, 18	Tacitus	
		10.97	17	*Annals*	
GL				15.2-8	40
2.7	68	Suetonius		15.44	40
2.9	68	*Claudius*			
2.25	23	25.4	39	*Hist.*	
				2.8	59

INDEX OF AUTHORS

Aune, D.E. 45

Bauckham, R.J. 56, 70
Bauer, W. 27
Bietenhard, H. 25, 44, 86, 92
Bori, P.C. 23, 25
Brown, R.E. 92
Burridge, K. 92

Caquot, A. 78
Chadwick, H. 27, 45
Charles, R.H. 14, 23-26, 55
Charlesworth, J.H. 56
Collins, A.Y. 41
Collins, J.J. 9, 15
Cullmann, O. 91

Daniélou, J. 9, 27, 55, 79, 92
De Ste Croix, G.E.M. 40-42
Donfried, K.P. 92
Dunn, J.D.G. 27, 91

Fitzmyer, J.A. 92
Flusser, D. 52
Frend, W.H.C. 27, 41, 42
Friedrich, G. 34, 46
Fuller, R. 91

Gager, J.G. 45
Graef, H.C. 92
Grant, R.M. 92
Gruenwald, I. 32, 67, 78, 80, 88, 89

Hahn, F. 91
Hall, R.G. 35, 66
Hanson, P.D. 27
Hedrick, C.W. 92

Helmbold, A.K. 90
Hill, D. 45
Hodgson, R. 92
Hurtado, L.W. 68, 80

Jeffers, J.S. 39, 57
Jonge, M. de 91

Klijn, A.F.J. 27
Knibb, M.A. 13, 14, 23-25, 48, 64, 78

Lampe, G.W. 45
Larkin, K.J. 27
Leonardi, C. 24
Longenecker, B.W. 27, 79

MacMullen, R. 46
Mannheim, K. 87
Markus, R.A. 46
Metzger, B.M. 24

Norelli, E. 56

Pesce, M. 14, 26, 35, 78

Reininck, G. 27
Reumann, J. 92
Robinson, J.M. 92
Rowland, C. 19, 27, 80, 81
Rudolph, K. 89, 92
Russell, D.S. 72

Schoedel, W.R. 27, 58
Smith, J.Z. 64, 80
Staniforth, M. 27
Stevenson, J. 17, 18, 27
Stone, M.E. 27, 69

Index of Authors

Strecker, G. 27

Ullendorff, E. 24

Vaillant, A. 25

Worsley, P. 92